100 GREATS

FEATHERSTONE ROVERS
RUGBY LEAGUE FOOTBALL CLUB

The agony and the ecstasy: Rovers players celebrate at the final whistle of the 1983 RL Cup Final at Wembley, in contrast to the Hull players.

Front cover: Deryck Fox in action for Great Britain. (Photograph courtesy of Varley Picture Agency.)

Back cover: Internationals Joe Mullaney (top), Don Fox (centre) and Jimmy Thompson (bottom).

100 GREATS

FEATHERSTONE ROVERS
RUGBY LEAGUE FOOTBALL CLUB

COMPILED BY
RON BAILEY

TEMPUS

Rovers' four Wembley captains meet together in 1996. From left to right: John Newlove (1973 and 1974), Eric Batten (1952), Terry Hudson (1983) and Malcolm Dixon (1967).

First published 2002

Tempus Publishing Limited
The Mill, Brimscombe Port,
Stroud, Gloucestershire, GL5 2QG

© Ron Bailey, 2002

British Library Cataloguing in Publication Data.
A catalogue record for this book is available from the British Library.

ISBN 0 7524 2713 X

Typesetting and origination by Tempus Publishing Limited
Printed in Great Britain by Midway Colour Print, Wiltshire

Introduction

In 2001 an Images of Sport publication chronicled the story of Featherstone Rovers since its admission to senior rugby league in 1921. That story covered its varied history of highs and lows set against the backcloth of a struggle for survival. This publication covers in greater detail some of the great players who were part of that story and their benign influence upon that struggle for survival.

From the beginning, the task of selecting 100 'great' players from the Rovers' 80 year history has been daunting and invidious. The only slight comfort is that this is not an exclusive selection, in the sense that the task has been to choose 'great', not the 'greatest', players. But what is great? The dictionary has many definitions – 'a high degree of magnitude', 'pre-eminent in genius', 'highly gifted', 'sublime', 'outstanding', 'swelling with emotion', 'favourite', 'excellent', 'on a large scale' and even 'pregnant'. At least the last definition could be discounted but all the rest, and their nuances, have to be considered. Furthermore, the research for this book has convinced me that a definition of greatness must include an understanding of the context and surrounding influences of an individual player's career, and this is especially important for a club whose playing strength has varied as much as Featherstone's. How do we judge the players whose performances were nurtured and conditioned in the glory years when Rovers challenged for League and Cup honours against the players whom fate decreed should sweat and toil in a poor side at the bottom of the league in the depressing 1930s? How do we weigh the standard of football being played from the variations of one league until 1973 and two divisions, three divisions, Super League and now the Northern Ford Premiership? Compensating judgements are required, but to what extent?

Then, of course, there is the inevitable issue of what criteria of greatness should be adopted. My initial thought was to record the number of club appearances as the main criterion, but how many make a 'great'? 100 appearances seemed reasonable, but a quick calculation revealed that there are possibly 130 players with that qualification. However, there are many Rovers players with fewer than 100 appearances who certainly made a great impact in shorter careers at the club. This applies particularly to those players who were transferred for financial reasons so that the club could survive. Then, developing the theme of survival, there were players who joined the club in the later stages of their own career, at bargain prices, but who left a considerable impression. These arguments dictate that a large number of appearances cannot be the sole criterion of greatness. Consequently, I determined that a player must have made at least fifty appearances for the club and have contributed significantly in some other way to be worthy of inclusion.

The other criteria employed in defining greatness are inevitably subjective and everyone will have their own views. Representative honours, points scoring records, defensive prowess, dependability, and the ability to influence one's peers are all important to varying degrees, together with my own assessment (as discussed above) of the broader context influencing the club at the time. This selection of 100 greats draws upon a range of evidence, from the club's own archives to material in private possession. Unusually, perhaps, I have trawled extensively through past editions of the *Pontefract and Castleford Express* and interviewed a number of players, relatives, coaches and commentators to supplement these sources. At this stage, one has also to mention that, regrettably, a lack of information and material had to have some bearing on the final selection. This particularly applies to the 1920s, 1930s and 1940s when sources are so limited. The likes of Wilf Evans (199 appearances), Charlie Hepworth (163), Luke Morgan (169), Wilf Pearson (155), G. Albert Taylor (161), George Taylor (293) and Bert Woolley (196), amongst others, must have played roles that could be deemed great, but the surviving evidence is too slim to assess or document their claims.

However, if selecting 100 greats had its problems, then having to select a top twenty from those players is even more daunting. A top thirty would have made that task easier because there is no doubt that players of the calibre of Tommy Askin, Eric Batten, Gary Jordan, Martin Pearson, Mick Smith, Charlie Stone, Walt Tennant and Brendon Tuuta, to name but a few, could have been included in a top twenty but there just wasn't enough space… Equally, there were many players on the fringe of the final 100 who were similarly affected, and consequently missed out on selection. Selectorial whim is the lot of all rugby players.

This task has provided a fascinating journey down memory lane, reliving the exploits of players who have helped shape the destiny of the club over the years. The final outcome shows a predominance towards the backs as against forwards which is understandable. The more interesting statistic is that 78 per cent of those selected began their Rovers careers from either junior (and mainly Featherstone juniors) or local rugby union teams. This endorses the fundamental point that Featherstone's survival has been entirely dependant on its own cradle of junior football. This has been and always will be the case, whether as a source of revenue to keep the wolves from the door or in providing a team capable of success. Another interesting point is that of the remaining 22 per cent, the majority were acquired from other clubs as 'bargain buys' in the transfer market and few of the expensive acquisitions feature in this list of 100 greats. The value and service of players like Albert Fearnley, Laurie Gant, Norman Hockley, Cyril Kellett, Freddie Miller, Steve Quinn, Tommy Smales and Cyril Woolford, who were all obtained at bargain prices, was immense, and has been as central to the club's survival as the sale of players like Karl Harrison and Graham Steadman who produced a substantial profit margin to the club.

Understandably, the 'impact' players dominate these 100 greats, but that does not belittle the efforts of the less conspicuous, solid and dependable players who played their part. Ultimately, this has to be a personal selection based on my own experiences and recollections, with no adverse implications for those who have not been included for whatever reason. I hope it represents a balanced list and that it will stimulate discussion! These players have certainly left their own legacies in the history of the club.

Ron Bailey
August 2002

Statistical Note

For my source of statistics, I have depended mainly on the records of Irvin Saxton, Stephen Parker, Chris Shaw and Terry Jones as my own records only extend to 1967. There have been the odd discrepancies but, by and large, the statistics quoted are accurate.

Any discrepancies are usually a function of variations in the record of appearances and scoring over the years. As far as appearances are concerned, the changes relate to the changing status of substitutes, from the initial reserve back (14) and reserve forward (15), introduced in 1964/65, to the bewildering inter-changing involving four substitutes within seventeen players in the modern game. Substitute appearances are included in brackets after the total appearances figure.

On scoring, since the value of drop goals was changed from two points to one, these goals have been separately listed. Prior to this change, the drop goals were included in the main goal lists and so, without extensive research, cannot be identified separately. For the points scorers, the increase in the value of a try from three to four points from 1983/84 needs acknowledging.

Acknowledgements

Most of the photographs used are from my own and the club's collections and have been built up from many sources over the years. These include the *Pontefract and Castleford Express*, Wakefield Express Series, *Yorkshire Post*, *Yorkshire Evening Post*, Provincial Press Agency, *Manchester Evening News*, *Sunday Pictorial*, *The Guardian*, Bradford & District Newspaper Co., and West Riding News Service, together with Eric Lorriman and Sig Kasatkin. I am indebted to all of these sources without whose help the story could not have been told. The exact origins of some photographs are unknown. If any copyright has been infringed, there has been no deliberate intent to do so.

I would also like to acknowledge my appreciation of the assistance from Terry Jones, the former chief executive of Featherstone Rovers, Irvin Saxton, Stephen Parker, Chris Shaw, Ken Everson, Jack Sykes, Terry Mullaney, Tony Collins, Steve Alderson, Donald Hunt, Mike McGowan and Andrew Howard. I am also grateful for the time spent and the memories shared with former players and colleagues including Keith Bell, Jack Blackburn, Mick Clamp, Malcolm Dixon, Vince Farrar, Peter Fox, Laurie Gant, Cliff Lambert, Joe Mullaney, John Newlove, Jimmy Thompson, Jim Williams, Gary Waterworth and Cyril Woolford.

Finally, as always, I am indebted to the support and patience of my family. To my wife Maureen who continues to encourage and type manuscripts so capably in the furtherance of my Rovers cause; and to our son Mark for his customary perceptive and analytical review.

All have contributed to support me in what has been a detailed and exhausting but nevertheless enjoyable journey through time, and I extend my sincere thanks to all.

100 Featherstone Greats

Dick Allman
Charlie Annable
Tommy Askin
Ralph Asquith
Alan Banks
Ernest Barraclough
Nigel Barker
Eric Batten
Keith Bell
Chris Bibb
Jack Blackburn
Harold Box
Keith Bridges
Ikram Butt
Richard Chapman
Mick Clamp
Terry Clawson
Billy Clements
Colin Clifft
Gary Cooper
Ray Cording
Keith Cotton
Paul Coventry
Jim Denton
Sid Denton
Malcolm Dixon
Carl Dooler
Ray Evans
Steve Evans
Vince Farrar
Willis Fawley
Albert Fearnley
Jack Fennell
Deryck Fox
Don Fox
Laurie Gant
Mick Gibbins

John Gilbert
Joe Golby
Jeff Grayshon
Ken Greatorex
Arthur Haigh
Karl Harrison
Dave Hartley
Frank Hemingway
Jack Higgins
Jack Hirst
David Hobbs
Norman Hockley
Terry Hudson
Fred Hulme
Jim Hunt
George Johnson
Gary Jordan
Cyril Kellett
Ken Kellett
Cliff Lambert
Ivor Lingard
Albany Longley
Paul Lyman
John Marsden
Don Metcalfe
Freddie Miller
Arnie Morgan
Joe Morgan
Percy Morris
Harold Moxon
Joe Mullaney
Steve Nash
John Newlove
Paul Newlove
Martin Pearson
Steve Quinn
Terry Ramshaw

Alan Rhodes
Jamie Rooney
Jimmy Russell
Bill Sherwood
Gary Siddall
Owen Simpson
Ian Smales
Tommy Smales
Mick Smith
Peter Smith
Graham Steadman
Richard Stone
Billy Stott
Arthur Street
Alan Tennant
Walt Tennant
Vaughan Thomas
Jimmy Thompson
Les Tonks
Brendon Tuuta
Gary Waterworth
Ken Welburn
Jimmy Williams
Arthur Wood
Cyril Woolford
Brian Wrigglesworth

The twenty who appear here in bold occupy two pages instead of the usual one.

Dick Allman
Stand Off/Centre, 1941-1949

Dick Allman was signed from Glasshoughton Juniors in June 1941 when the Rovers were playing in the War Emergency League. He made his senior debut on 6 September v. Keighley (at home), marking his debut with a try. He followed this with two tries in each of the next two matches and five tries in three games was an auspicious start. In a shortened season, he appeared in eight of the Rovers' league and cup games without adding to his try tally.

He featured strongly in the remainder of the war years, eventually making 59 appearances in the Emergency Leagues. He switched from centre to the stand-off position in 1943, which many considered his best position.

Eagerly awaiting the resumption of peacetime football in August 1945, Allman was the lynch pin of the Rovers backs as the team made an excellent start. By November, only three of thirteen league games had been lost, the Rovers were challenging for the 'Top Four' and their backs had scored 32 of the 35 tries scored. This was a tribute to the inventive play of Allman at number 6, whose influence was typified on 24 November 1945 by a brilliant performance in the 8-4 victory at Rochdale which put Rovers in third position. Unfortunately, two weeks later he damaged his shoulder at Bradford and the injury was to keep him out for the rest of the season. It was no coincidence that the fortunes of the side, deprived of its influential half back, changed dramatically. The team lost 14 of the next 18 league and cup games, ending the season in 13th position.

He resumed in the 1946/47 season making most appearances (31) by a back. In difficult times as the team languished near the foot of the table, his play was invariably characterised by full eighty-minute displays. He was solid and dependable in defence and attack. The only blip in his career was in early 1948, when Gilbertson was signed from Dewsbury and temporarily displaced him. The club refused his request to be transfer-listed and he then refused to play v. Hull (at home) and was suspended for two weeks. He put this dispute behind him in the following season, when he

reaffirmed that his talent made him one of the mainstays of the team, again making most appearances by a back (33). His half-back partnership with Jimmy Russell was a particular feature.

Sadly his career was cut short when, after only four appearances in the new season, he received an ankle injury in the Yorkshire Cup game at Wakefield on 10 September 1949. This injury necessitated an operation and ended his career. His contribution in the difficult years of the 1940s was characterised by tenacity and dedication, so that Dick Allman made the most of his talent and became the solid, reliable player which every club needs.

Total appearances: 164   Tries: 32   Goals: 4   Points: 104

Charlie Annable
Scrum-Half, 1924-31

Jeff Moores, the Australian centre who joined Leeds in 1927, referred to Annable as 'the smartest half back I have seen either in my own country or England' after his first game against the Rovers in the Yorkshire Cup game at Headingley on 8 October 1927. Rovers lost 10-2 and Annable fractured his collar bone, but Moores had seen enough and knew that here was a star in the making. Ironically, that season was to be the worst in Annable's Rovers career. He resumed playing a month later and inspired Rovers to a 15-3 win over St Helens, but he then damaged the same shoulder and was out for the rest of the season. This meant that he missed the League Championship play-offs and his absence was particularly notable in the final, which Rovers lost 11-0. How they needed his artistry to unlock the Swinton defence.

Signed from Alverthorpe in September 1924, Annable made his senior debut *v*. Hull KR (at home) on 27 September. He was an instant success and opened his try scoring account in his second match, with two tries against Wyke in the Yorkshire Cup. He played in 36 of the 37 remaining fixtures.

Annable struck up a remarkable half back partnership with Jimmy Williams, which was a major feature of the Featherstone set-up from 1924 to 1929 when Williams was transferred to York. His effervescent back play (he was described as always appearing so 'excitable' on field) sparked off many memorable tries and matches. At home to Salford on 31 October 1925 he 'bamboozled the Salford defence' with two tries which inspired a 22-15 win; at home to Castleford in November 1928 he 'went round the pack with a glorious dummy' to score the try which led to a 10-6 win and Rovers' first appearance in a Yorkshire Cup final; and on 18 January 1930, in one of the most thrilling matches seen at Post Office Road, Annable prompted Rovers to a 15-14 win over Hunslet after which the team were chaired from the field.

Annable's form warranted representative honours, but his career coincided with that of the great Jonty Parkin of Wakefield. After being selected in the Yorkshire shadow team, his patience was finally rewarded in 1929 when he played against Glamorgan/Monmouthshire in April, scoring a try and creating another in Yorkshire's 22-17 win. In November he played against the Australian tourists.

With the departure of Williams, Annable found a new partner towards the end of season 1929/30 in the seventeen-year-old discovery, Billy Stott – although the partnership was threatened by the announcement that 'on financial grounds with the view of reducing debt, the club has transfer-listed the finest scrum-half to play for this club'. There were no immediate takers and Annable enjoyed a full season with the highly promising Stott.

Annable's form was outstanding at the beginning of the 1931/32 season, and he was described as 'brilliant' in the home defeat by Leeds. He played at Hull on 12 September 1931, but was then transferred to Castleford for £400. His outstanding talent had ensured that Rovers' fight for survival had again been eased. He made 30 appearances for Castleford from 1931 to 1933.

Total appearances: 196   Tries: 29   Goals: 2   Points: 91

Tommy Askin

Centre, 1924-29 & 1938-39

Although selected as a winger for the 1928 tour of Australasia, Tommy Askin only played five games on the wing during a Rovers career of 130 appearances; he played the rest of his matches as a centre. He made his senior debut on 21 March 1925 at Dewsbury, where he scored his first try, and he finished the season with 3 tries in 8 appearances. He made sufficient impression to be described at the annual general meeting as 'another Hirst', which was praise indeed. That initial promise was fulfilled and in 1925/26 he played in 35 of the club's 36 fixtures and only missed the Salford game because he had been involved in a motor accident. He scored 13 tries and his centre partnership with Jack Hirst made them a formidable duo.

His scintillating play demanded recognition and on 16 September 1927 he played his first game for Yorkshire against Glamorgan /Monmouthshire at Hunslet. Unfortunately, this appearance only lasted ten minutes as he was kicked on the head and had to be taken to hospital for stitches. He eventually made four appearances. In February the trial games for the 1928 tour were played. Askin played at centre in the second trial and scored a try. He was not included in the tour party which was announced after the game, but two vacancies were left open – for a winger and a forward. Interestingly, the Rovers then selected him on the wing for three matches and he scored two tries away to Salford. The selectors then added him to the tour party, and, almost in celebration, he scored three tries against York on 7 April – this time as a centre!

Although there was not much money in Featherstone, the community was proud of the club's first tourist and they sent him off on tour with a complete outfit – handsome cabin trunk and suitcase and everything likely to wear – including a suit of plus fours. He was one of the outstanding successes and he showed his versatility by playing in the wing, centre and stand-off positions and scoring 9 tries in 15 appearances; he played in all three Tests against both Australia and New Zealand.

He missed his club's involvement in the League Championship play-offs in April and May, and did not return to England until

September. He received a great ovation in his first match at home to York on 6 October, but received a knee injury which put him out of action for seven matches. He managed to appear in the ill-fated 1928 Yorkshire Cup final against Leeds, but had to withdraw through injury from the England team v. Wales in November. After playing at Dewsbury on 29 December, he did not play in the return fixture at Featherstone on New Year's Day. The report said that 'he was in the midst of difficulties with the committee'. The upshot was that he was transfer-listed and signed for Leeds in February 1929. The fee of £800 was a club record and, yet again, eased the financial situation.

With Leeds he made 42 appearances (17 tries) before being transferred to Castleford in 1930. There he continued his try scoring prowess with 64 tries in 196 appearances and played in the winning RL Cup Final side of 1935. In 1937 he had a brief loan at new club Newcastle before he finally returned to Post Office Road in October 1938, making his return against, yes, Dewsbury. He played twelve matches, his last game being at home to Leigh on 28 January 1939.

Total appearances: 130   Tries: 45   Goals: 1   Points: 137

Ralph Asquith
Winger, 1933-39

The 1930s were undoubtedly one of the worst periods in the club's history. From 1933 to 1938 the team languished near the foot of the league table, and in two seasons had over 800 points scored against them – 804 in 1934/35 and 858 in 1936/37. Playing for the Rovers at that time could not have been much fun but one player who shone in this period was Ralph Asquith. Signed from Featherstone Juniors in October 1933, he made his debut v. Hull KR on 11 October. He scored his first try in his second game v. Hull at home on 4 November 1933. His sheer pace and determination promised a bright future.

At the end of his first season, he had scored 4 tries in 19 appearances. He was injured towards the end and so missed the game at Bramley on 3 April 1934, when the Rovers won 7-0. Almost three years elapsed before the next away league victory when, on 7 March 1937, a surprise 16-9 win was obtained at Leigh. Ralph Asquith scored three of the four tries on that day to play his part in such

a welcome victory. He was the club's leading try scorer on three occasions in 1935/36 (8 tries), 1937/38 (9) and 1938/39 (11). The try that must have given him the greatest satisfaction was scored on 24 February 1934. The Rovers (bottom of the league) were playing Leeds (who were lying in fifth place) and in one of the most thrilling matches seen at Post Office Road, they produced a brilliant game of football in which 14 tries were scored with Leeds winning 33-23. The best of several excellent tries came towards the end when sterling approach work left young Asquith to beat renowned internationals Jim Brough and Stan Smith. This he did magnificently and the Rovers left the field to a 'storm of cheers in recognition of a great performance'.

His unenviable claim to fame was on 21 September 1935 when the Rovers were heavily defeated 60-2 by Huddersfield at Fartown. Playing opposite Asquith was Ray Markham, who scored a record nine tries. Asquith never forgot that game but, like the rest of the Rovers players in this difficult period, he had to persevere tenaciously on slender resources and did so creditably.

Ironically, just as the tide was starting to turn, Asquith was struck by tragedy. In 1937 the committee pledged a new policy of retaining players and signed on fourteen new players. The reward was the best playing record since 1932 in 1938/39 with 13 victories and 2 drawn games in the league programme. Asquith had his best seasonal try tally of 11 in 31 appearances. The future looked rosy, but in June his career was to be shattered. He lost the sight in one eye when fragments of steel entered his eye in an accident at work. His last game was away to St Helens on 29 April 1939. His devotion to the Rovers cause then took a different turn when he replaced his father as a guarantor on the Rovers committee in 1944, serving for almost thirty years. He was elected vice-chairman in 1962 and died suddenly as he prepared to attend the Rovers game against the Australian Tourists on 18 November 1972.

Total appearances: 158   Tries: 43   Goals: 2   Points: 133

Alan Banks

Alan Banks shared a family pedigree for rugby league football. His younger brother Keith played for Wakefield Trinity, and his other brother, Barry, played for York and Hull. It was not surprising therefore that Alan was outstanding at schoolboy and junior level and he was snapped up by the Rovers from their Under-17 side at the tender age of seventeen years. He was signed as a stand-off and made his full senior debut away to Hull on 10 November 1982. Despite his youth, he soon displayed his talent and scored his first try in the Boxing Day home victory over Carlisle. When the 1983 RL Challenge Cup trail began, he was thrust into the epic 11-10 win at St Helens in the third round followed by the semi-final win over Bradford. This was 'blooding' indeed and his reward was a Wembley appearance seven days before his eighteenth birthday. He was certainly the youngest Rovers player to have appeared at Wembley and at the time he was the second youngest ever – Reg Lloyd of Keighley was 17 years 7 months old when he played in the 1937 final.

His progress continued and in the following season he had an uninterrupted run of 38 consecutive matches which ran into September 1984 and he was proving to be a very effective partner to Deryck Fox. His versatility began to emerge when he success-fully switched to centre in December. He was then back at stand-off and alternated comfort-ably between the two positions to suit the needs of the club. With the arrival of Graham Steadman in February 1986, he settled in the centre but after playing at St Helens in January 1987, he was out of the game for over a year. He returned at Oldham in February 1988 at centre, and soon showed that he had lost none of his skills. Indeed, he moved into probably his best period with the club, enjoying his best season in 1988/89 playing in all 35 matches. He was again dominant in the following season, playing in 34 of the 36 games and even appearing at full-back and on the wing – thus qualifying as a utility back. He also received the Keith Goulding Clubman of the Year award in May 1990, which demonstrated the esteem in which he was held. After the euphoria of Wembley in 1983, he had to share the partial disappointment of being runners-up in the Second Division trophy v. Oldham in 1988 and the Yorkshire Cup v. Bradford in 1989.

With the acquisition of players of the calibre of Newlove, Simpson, Bibb and Smales, Banks did not play for the club as frequently in 1990/91, but in his utility back role he scored five tries in eight games. It was, however, a complete surprise when he decided to retire at the comparatively early age of twenty-five after playing at Warrington on 20 January 1991.

With his early entry into senior football, he had played eight seasons. Averaging nearly thirty appearances a season and renowned for his fearless and solid defence, he was a consis-tent and highly committed player. Alan Banks was a fine reader of the game, supporting play shrewdly and effectively in attack, and was a very good ambassador for the club both on and off the field.

Total appearances: 218 (+15)   Tries: 46   Points: 182

Nigel Barker

Full Back, 1980-91

The familiar saying 'If at first you don't succeed, try try again' could well have been applied to Nigel Barker who thrilled the Rovers supporters in the 1980s. However, it could have been a different story if he had not persisted with his career and desire to play for the club. He played with Featherstone Juniors in the forwards, but at the Under 19 stage he was advised to play open age football to develop his game. He joined the Featherstone Miners Welfare club and eventually settled into the full-back position. His displays began to interest senior clubs, but he was still intent on playing for his home club. He signed in December 1980 at the comparatively ripe old age of twenty-five, but it did not take him too long to make up for lost time.

He made his senior debut on 25 January 1981 at home to Hull when John Marsden, the current incumbent of the number one jersey, was injured. It was not until the beginning of the next season, however, that he was able to establish himself properly. Selected for the opening game of the season

with Castleford, he took the opportunity in fine style and played in all 34 games that season. His first tries (a brace) were scored in the 36-9 home win over York on 15 November 1981 and his fine run of consecutive appearances continued into the 1982/83 season. The run ended at 47 appearances, but he only missed 3 of the 37 games played that season. In February 1983, after a comfortable 21-5 first round win over Batley, it was hard to envisage that the Rovers were on the verge of another historic RL Cup run. A second round encounter at Salford was formidable and, in an absorbing tussle, the Rovers withstood everything Salford threw at them and produced their own Man of the Match in Nigel Barker. Apart from his defensive stint, twice he ran from deep and waltzed through the Salford defence to score two match-winning tries in a 17-11 victory. Two more epic games followed against St Helens (11-10) and Bradford (11-6) in the semi-final. In both games, Barker was described as a 'tower of strength', showing to the full his main attributes of a superb defence, masterly under the high ball, and proficient at bringing the ball away from his line. Wembley crowned what probably ranks as his best season (with his highest seasonal try tally of 10).

He continued to hold the number one spot and had another successful season in 1985/86, when again, he featured in all 34 games in the season – this was quite an achievement. The following year, Chris Bibb came to the fore and Barker's appearances began to diminish. His last full game in the senior team was at home to Wigan on 1 March 1989, although he did appear as a substitute in the match at home to Warrington on 16 April 1989. He then concentrated on passing his experience on in the 'A' team until 1991, by which time he had completed 10 years service with the club, and was granted a testimonial. A Rovers career which had begun relatively late thus came to an end at the age of thirty-six, an achievement which demonstrates the persistence, dedication and talent which Nigel Barker brought to the club.

Total appearances: 175 (+23)　　　Tries: 28　　　Points: 100

Ernest Barraclough

Prop Forward, 1921-34

Ernest Barraclough was one of the elite thirteen who represented Featherstone Rovers in their first game in senior rugby league at Bradford on 27 August 1921. He was, however, the only one of those players who was injured in that game and he had to miss the next two games. This absence for two games did not matter too much, however, as he went on to amass a total of 435 appearances for the club in a career which spanned from 1921 to 1934 – the most ever by a Rovers forward and only five behind the all-time appearances total of 440 by Jim Denton. Yet, if one analyses Barraclough's phenomenal record, he could easily have gained the all-time record for himself had it not been for a lively personal disposition. As a prop forward, he was always in the thick of the action, which resulted in several 'early baths' and resultant suspensions. According to newspaper reports, he missed seventeen matches through suspension and eleven through being in dispute with the committee!

His remarkable record of consistency made him the mainstay of the Rovers pack in those formative years following admission to the league. He scored his first try on 30 September 1922 in his 38th game for the club and his best try tally in a season was six in 1927/28. This was one of his best seasons when he suffered mixed fortunes. His form was such that many tipped him for a place on the 1928 tour of Australasia, and he was disappointed that he was not even selected for the tour trial matches. Shortly afterwards, he was sent off at Hunslet in March and the resultant four match suspension brought an end to a record run of 54 consecutive matches. Those four matches were the only games he missed in a crowded season.

Representative honours did come his way. He was selected for the Yorkshire side which faced Lancashire in November 1924, but had to withdraw through injury. Happily, he made his debut almost a year later against Lancashire and Cumberland. He featured in the success enjoyed in those early years – the epic second round RL Cup tie with Wigan in March 1923; the successful league campaign of 1927/28 which culminated in a rousing championship semi-final defeat of Leeds at Headingley, but a disappointing final against Swinton; and the equally disappointing first ever Yorkshire Cup final against Leeds in November 1928 which also ended in defeat. Inevitably, whenever the Rovers carried off astounding victories in their first decade where the foundation of the victory had been laid by the heroes of the pack, then it was usually Ernest Barraclough who was to the fore. Apart from his presence and power, he was particularly famous for his dribbles with the ball at his feet, a feature of the game in the pre-war years.

His sheer consistency and durability amazed Rovers supporters. After playing at Widnes on 14 April 1934, he allegedly announced his retirement. The Rovers, however, retained him on their register and when Broughton Rangers offered £100 in August he was transferred there.

Total appearances: 435   Tries: 21   Points: 63

Eric Batten
Winger, 1951-56

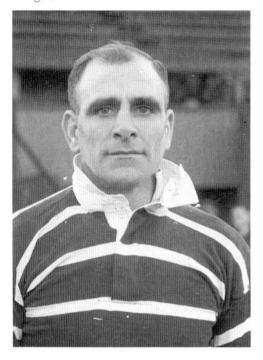

Eric Batten was already a rugby league legend when he joined Featherstone as player-coach from Bradford Northern in June 1951. The second son of the famous Billy Batten, he had played with Wakefield, Hunslet and Bradford and won almost every honour in the game with appearances for Yorkshire, England and Great Britain, a Lions tour of Australasia and League Championship, RL Cup and Yorkshire Cup final medals. Described as 'the strongest and most virile winger', he was a prolific try scorer and, like his father, developed the skill of leaping clean over opponents who went in for a low tackle.

When he joined Rovers at the age of thirty-six, the club was attempting to pull out of the doldrums. There was a nucleus of young promising talent which benefited from Batten's experience and methods with remarkable effect. He believed that hard training was the key to success, and he transmitted this philosophy to his players.

He made his debut at home to Rochdale on 18 August 1951. The match report said 'little was seen of Batten until eight minutes from time when he showed that all he wanted was the opportunity and his purposeful dash gave Kent a try ... and he then scored a try to deprive Rochdale of victory'. Indeed, he scored 17 tries in that season, a total only one short of Jack Hirst's record of 18 in 1922/23.

With his inspiration and direction the Rovers began to move up the league table but it was their exploits in the 1952 RL Cup which set the RL world alight. Opening victories against Rochdale and Batley were followed by the historic third round, 14-11 defeat of the mighty Wigan on 15 March 1952, one of the biggest Cup shocks of all time. Batten's 400th career try late in the game helped seal the victory. Another shock win over Leigh in the semi-final sent Rovers to their first ever RL Cup Final. It was a record fourth Wembley appearance for Eric and although he scored yet another memorable try, illustrating his unfailing prowess, the Rovers lost 18-10, but gained the plaudits for their contribution to an excellent final. Batten's style of coaching – fitness allied with brilliant defensive work, backed by burning spirit and enthusiasm – had been justified and the stamina and fitness of the team was acclaimed.

Inevitably he set up a new club record of 26 tries in season 1952/53 in 37 appearances. 17 more tries followed in 1953/54, but after playing at Hull in September 1954, he announced his retirement from playing to concentrate on coaching. The Rovers then progressed to ninth position in 1954/55, their highest position since 1928 and reached the RL Cup semi-final; and finished sixth in 1955/56. However, the club then appointed Bill Hudson as coach and thus ended an extraordinary five years with the club. As a coach, he had ignited the talent which was to lead to even better things; as a player he concluded a remarkable career in incredible style. To score 60 tries in 101 games in his late thirties and to amass a career total of 435 tries in 630 games was the perfect testimony to his fitness, dedication and talent.

Total appearances: 101   Tries: 60   Points: 180

16

Keith Bell
Utility Forward, 1971-90

Keith Bell's father and three brothers all played for Featherstone Rovers and so it seems that he was destined not only to play rugby league but also to play for the Rovers. He signed as a hooker from Featherstone juniors team, and made his senior debut at home to Batley on 28 November 1971, when he scored a try in a 54-0 demolition. Keith Bridges was the Featherstone number 9 at that time and a player from whom Bell learned a great deal. Nevertheless, this meant that young Bell had to bide his time. He made only five senior appearances in that first season, but was able to be a part of the successful 'A' team which won the Yorkshire Senior Competition Championship. The following season was again spent deputising for Bridges, but on 12 November 1972 the coach, Peter Fox, decided to play him at loose forward. Although this was his only appearance that season at number 13, there were many more appearances to come in that position and many more drop goals.

After this brief excursion into the number 13 jersey, he returned to his number 9 position, deputising until Peter Fox gave him his second opportunity at loose-forward – in the Captain Morgan Trophy final on 26 January 1974, ahead of 'Charlie' Stone. Although the Rovers lost 4-0, he played impressively and for the rest of the season was either deputising for Bridges or vying with Stone. It certainly showed his blossoming versatility. When the Rovers commenced another splendid RL Cup run, he secured the number 13 spot and was delighted to appear in the 1974 final at Wembley. Although Warrington once again dashed the Rovers' hopes, it was a marvellous experience for Bell in only his third season.

He still floated between the two positions in 1974/75, but new coach Keith Goulding decided that Bell's talents were to be best utilised in any of the back three positions. That's where he was put and that's where he stayed from 1975 to 1983, giving Bell the opportunity to revel as a master tactician and ball handler. In 1975/76, he only missed two matches and scored his highest seasonal total of tries, 12. This season also saw the birth of that redoubtable pack combination

of Thompson, Bridges, Farrar, Smith, Stone and Bell which was to form the basis of future Rovers success. Not that it helped in the 1976 Yorkshire Cup final, which Leeds won 16-12, and proved to be another disappointment for Bell.

Recompense came at the end of the 1976/77 season, when a very competent Rovers outfit were crowned First Division Champions for the first time in their history. Bell played his full part by making 36 appearances, and further rewards came later in 1977. He made his Yorkshire County debut v. Cumberland at York in October – the first of four appearances. On 12 November he played for the Great Britain Under 24 team against France at Hull. Great Britain won 27-9 and a month later won the return encounter at Tonneins. He scored the winning try there and took the Man of the Match Award in both games. The match reports focused upon his intelligent passing and tricky breaks, attributes which the Featherstone fans knew all about. However, a Yorkshire Cup winners' medal still evaded him as Rovers lost their second successive final, this time to Castleford.

With the break-up of that famous pack, only Bell and Peter Smith remained as the 'veterans' around which a new pack was to be built. Bell's

---

Total appearances: 391 (+26)   Tries: 57   Goals: 1   Drop Goals: 73   Points: 265

Keith Bell scores one of the tries in Rovers' 33-7 RL Cup victory over Leeds on 14 March 1977, their highest third round score.

experience was invaluable as he continued to add to his own personal performances in appearances and drop goals which had become his particular speciality. He had three drop goals in two games *v.* Hull (at home) in August 1979 and in January 1981 at Bradford. In that season, 1980/81, he drop kicked 15 goals, all of which must have been records in their own right, at the time.

In May 1982, the local *Express* reported that Rovers' back three of 'Smith, Hobbs and Bell were the envy of the Rugby League'. One year later, he experienced one of his worst disappointments when coach Alan Agar did not include him in the Rovers XV which triumphed over Hull in the RL Cup Final. Nor did he feature much in the following season, 1983/84; indeed, he only made three appearances in what was his testimonial season, although it was his thirteenth year with the club.

He returned to the fold properly in 1985/86, operating mainly in the second row; 12 drop goals in 23 appearances showed that his flair and opportunism still had a part to play. However, in 1986/87, the Rovers slid into the Second Division for the second time in his career (1978/79 was the first occasion). Fortunately, they bounced back at the first attempt at a time when Bell had returned to the hooking role. The team finished second in the league table, but lost the Premiership Trophy Final to Oldham by 28 points to 26. This was his last big stage. He continued to make the odd appearance with the seniors until 1990 (his last match being at home to Wigan in March) and he was given a free transfer in November. His Rovers career had spanned 19 years and six months, a record for any Rovers player, and his career 73 drop goals must also be a record. He then joined Hunslet, where he made 60 appearances before finally retiring in 1993 at the age of thirty-nine years.

Keith Bell was considered by many to be one of the finest ball-handlers in the game. With his intelligent approach, he was a quick thinker, a superb footballer and could read the game. His astute passing and kicking oiled Rovers' attacking play for years. He graced the game and the club he loved so well – indeed there can have been no better clubman.

Chris Bibb
Full-Back, 1985-94

Signed in June 1985 from Lock Lane, Chris Bibb made two substitute appearances in 1985/86 before his full senior debut *v.* St Helens (at home) on 9 November 1986 – but on the wing! The following match he was in his own position of full-back at a time when he was in competition with Nigel Barker. His form was sufficient to gain selection for Great Britain Colts against France in Toulouse in February 1987, and a month later he played for the Great Britain Under 21 team against France at St Helens and St Jean de Luc. He was to make three more appearances for the Under 21 team in 1985 and 1989.

Back on the home front, he established himself in the number 1 shirt from the 1987/88 season as he developed into one of the most exciting full-backs seen at Post Office Road. He had a safe pair of hands and was extremely quick which, combined with an elusive swerve, made him very difficult to stop at speed. With Peter Fox as coach, a particular move was developed whereby the ball would be kicked from a scrum into open space for Bibb to chase, and he was also able to link readily with the back line to devastating effect. The result was a series of dazzling displays with some spectacular tries. In 1987/88, he scored 20 tries including three against Rochdale (at home) in September, and he followed this with 13 in 1988/89 and 16 the following season. Particularly memorable were the efforts at Wakefield in January 1989 with an eighty-yard touchline dash; at Wigan in April 1989, when he picked up a loose ball fifteen yards from his line and scythed his way through to score; in October 1989, when his stunning solo try against Castleford in the Yorkshire Cup semi-final enabled Rovers to draw 18-18 at home and win the replay at Castleford; and his six tries in the Yorkshire Cup game with Keighley in September 1989, when he equalled the match try scoring record held by Mick Smith since 1968. There are many more examples of his attacking qualities and, rightly, more representative honours followed. He had an outstanding debut for Yorkshire in their crushing 56-12 win over Lancashire at Wigan

in September 1989, when he scored, and an equally impressive display in his second game *v.* Lancashire in September 1991 when he again scored in Yorkshire's 17-12 win. He also gained senior international honours in 1990 when he replaced Steve Hampson on the Great Britain tour of Papua New Guinea and New Zealand. He made eight appearances on tour, scoring one try and playing in the First Test *v.* New Zealand at Palmerston North.

In such a success story, there were still some disappointments. He missed out through injury in the Second Division Premiership Trophy Finals in 1988 and 1993, and shared the disappointment of defeat in the 1989 Yorkshire Cup final against Bradford. The club suffered relegation to the Second Division in 1991/92 – the season in which Bibb made the most appearances (36) and scored another 11 tries.

In 1994, Bibb had his differences with the club and he was transfer-listed at £90,000. He played his last game at home against Salford on 24 April. He was granted a testimonial in 1995 and then drifted out of the game. To some observers he never quite fulfilled the undoubted talent he had, but 76 career tries is a remarkable record for a full-back and speaks volumes for his thrilling performances for the club.

Total appearances: 213 (4)   Tries: 76   Goals: 6   Points: 316

Jack Blackburn
Winger/Full-Back, 1939-53

June. He scored a try in both the first and second round wins over Halifax and Bradford, and was elated to be in the Rovers team which won the Cup on 22 June 1940, the club's first ever senior trophy – all this at barely eighteen years of age.

War had, however, been declared in September 1939, which meant that at a time when he could have been developing his career he had to serve in the Royal Air Force. As such, he was only able to make six appearances for his club from 1942 to 1946. He played rugby union in the RAF, during which time he fractured both his jaw and collar bone. It was the shoulder injury which was to carry an unfortunate legacy. Resuming his Rovers career in December 1946, he alternated between playing on the wing and as a full-back. In 1948, however, he suffered further disruption when his collar bone was fractured on three occasions, leading him to consider retiring from the game.

With typical grit and determination, he began his comeback in September 1949, having been out for almost a year, and managed 19 appearances in that season – his highest total in ten years. He battled on, showing the deft touches which had always characterised his game, and was described thus: 'although handicapped by slight of build he was one of the most stylish of players. Fast, a safe catcher and tackler and accurate goal-kicker'. His football brain was exceptional and his ankle tackling was distinctive and exemplary. In 1951 he was granted a joint testimonial with Jimmy Russell, the Rovers scrum-half, and they each received £216 in 1952. By that time, Featherstone had been to Wembley, but there was no place for him in the Cup squad. Ironically, after making 20 appearances in the 1952/53 season, his highest ever total, he was not retained at the end of that season and he retired at the age of thirty-one. His last match was at Hunslet in May 1953. One could not help wondering, however, of what might have been if his career had flown more freely. His courage and persistence deserved more.

Jack Blackburn was one of the unluckiest players at Featherstone. He had tremendous talent, made a bright start to his career, which underlined that talent, and then experienced a series of frustrating disruptions. He played his junior football with another Rovers great, Walt Tennant, in the highly successful Girnhill Lane team which only lost two matches in two years. At the tender age of sixteen he made his first appearance for Rovers in August 1938 in the charity game with Castleford. He played at centre and his opponent was Arthur Atkinson, Castleford's international centre. Rovers wanted to sign him then, but he considered he was too young.

He eventually signed in late 1939 and made his official senior debut on the wing away to Bramley in December. What a first season he had! In 15 appearances he scored 9 tries, including his first hat-trick, *v*. Keighley in May 1940, which was fine tuning for the historic Yorkshire Cup run which emerged in

---

Total appearances: 139   Tries: 29   Goals: 38   Points: 163

Harold Box

How about kicking six goals out of ten at the age of seventeen on your senior debut? That was the remarkable introduction to his Rovers career by Harold Box at home to Keighley on 17 January 1970. He had joined the club from Fryston Juniors in June 1969 when veteran full-back Cyril Kellett was still in command. He thus spent his first season in the 'A' team, but when Cyril broke his ankle in January 1970 it gave Harold his chance. Ironically, he had only turned to goal-kicking in the 'A' team because of problems over a consistent goal-kicker and he soon mastered the art. With Cyril out for the rest of the season, he had an unbroken run of fifteen appearances but for the next four seasons he vied with him for the full-back position. He missed out in the Yorkshire Cup final *v.* Leeds in 1970 and the RL Cup Final *v.* Bradford in 1973, but took the number 1 spot in the Captain Morgan Trophy Final and RL Cup Final in 1974, both against Warrington.

When Kellet retired in May 1974, Box had chalked up 40 appearances out of 45 that season, and kicked 92 goals – his best ever season for both. He appeared consistently at full-back from 1974 to 1980, but the arrival of Steve Quinn in January 1976 restricted his goal kicking. His best goal kicking feat was nine goals, achieved twice, against Batley (at home) in November 1971, and against Halifax (at home) in January 1973.

He was qualified to play for Wales and played in the European Championship games *v.* France and England in both 1979 and 1980. Many thought that his form warranted inclusion in the 1979 tour to Australia and New Zealand, but George Fairbairn of Wigan gained selection instead. He made his debut for Yorkshire in 1979 playing against Cumberland in August and Lancashire in September, his only appearances.

On the club front, there were contrasting emotions as he shared the ecstasy of being First Division champions in 1976/77; and the despair of another Yorkshire Cup final defeat in 1976 and relegation to the Second Division in 1978/79. At least in that season he was rewarded with the John Jepson trophy for

Player of the Season – and he did play his part in the Rovers' immediate return to the First Division, as Second Division champions in 1979/80.

He was granted a testimonial in 1979/80 and the supporters responded with a then record of £5,751. For many fans it was acknowledgement of the part which he had played through the fluctuating 1970s. A slow starter, he took time to develop but the finished product was a solid, strong and reliable full-back whose attributes were a safe defence; flair in attack; effective support and link play; power and pace (witness his three tries in the Yorkshire Cup game at home to Huddersfield in August 1978); and sound positional sense which meant he always appeared to be in the right place at the right time. Above all, he always displayed character and determination which made him a firm favourite with the fans. His last match was at home to Whitehaven in March 1980 and he was transferred to Wakefield Trinity in September 1980 for £18,000.

Senior appearances: 274 (+9)   Tries: 57   Goals: 476   Points: 1123

John Howard (Keith) Bridges
Hooker, 1969-79

Like father like son! John Howard Bridges is the son of Keith Bridges, who made 110 appearances for Castleford between 1957 and 1963 and was a more than average hooker. John Howard followed in his father's footsteps in the hooking position, but joined the Rovers from Featherstone juniors. Despite his given name, he also inherited his father's 'Keith'!

As good as his father was, even he would admit that his son was one of the best in the game. Without exception, he was regarded as one of the fastest hookers at a time when hookers were the major source of possession. Indeed, he was so fast at striking for the ball in the scrum that team-mates would swear that often referees would penalise him unjustly because they considered he had gained the ball illegally. Having signed for the Rovers in January 1969, he faced initial competition for the number 9 slot from Vince Farrar and Dennis Morgan and he did not make his first senior appearance until August 1970, when he came on as a substitute against Wigan. His full senior debut came five days later on 31 August 1960 at Castleford. It was not until the end of that season that he established himself as the first choice hooker and from then he never looked back.

His reputation grew with his consistency in the early 1970s and the possession he gained for his side undoubtedly helped the Rovers to move up into the top echelons of the league table from 1972. His general play earned him many Man of the Match awards. When the Rovers began their RL Cup trail in 1973, they were drawn against the all-star Salford side in the first round. The Post Office Road crowd witnessed a spectacle as the Rovers had to pull out all the stops to prevent their talented opponents taking command. That they achieved this was partly due to the overwhelming scrum possession – Bridges heeled all twelve scrums in the first half, and although it levelled at 4-4 in the second half, the damage had been done and Rovers won 18-11. They progressed to the final to beat Bradford 33-14 in what was to be Keith's only winning Cup medal with the Rovers. He played in the 1974 RL Cup Final and the Captain Morgan Trophy final against Warrington, as well as the Yorkshire Cup final against Leeds in 1976, but lost on each occasion.

Such form brought its due reward in representative recognition when he played for Great Britain in France at Grenoble on 20 January 1974, and was retained for the return fixture at Wigan a month later when he was reported as the best tackler in the match, as well as giving Great Britain the edge in the scrums. Having suitably impressed, he was selected for the 1974 tour of Australasia, but injured his knee in the First Test v. Australia at Brisbane, which curtailed his tour to eight appearances. He underwent a cartilage operation in September and was out of action until December, but returned with all his old verve and skill to play in six of England's eight games in the World Championship of 1975. England finished runners-up to Australia in the final table. On the County side, he represented Yorkshire on five occasions between October 1975 and October 1977.

On the home front, the famous front row of Thompson, Bridges and Farrar made their first appearance as a unit for Rovers in 1975 and helped sweep the club from runners-up in

---

Total appearances: 232 (+3)   Tries: 44   Goals: 5   Drop goals: 3   Points: 145

Keith Bridges is carried from the Wembley field by Peter Small and Jimmy Williams, after being concussed in the 1973 RL Cup Final between Rovers and Bradford Northern.

1975/76 to First Division champions in 1976/77. He only missed three games in the championship season, his best ever for the club. After the euphoria of that magnificent season, the bubble burst with the departure of Thompson and Farrar and a year later Keith severed his ties with the club he had served so well. Injured in the opening game of season 1978/79 at home to Huddersfield in the Yorkshire Cup game on 20 August 1978, the resultant knee ligament operation kept him out for the rest of the season. He had resumed training in the close season of 1979 when Bradford Northern made contact and he was transferred for £23,000. It was reckoned that the only hooker who could compete with him was Ray Hanscombe and when Bridges left, the club signed Hanscombe. Bridges moved from Bradford to Hull in July 1982 and ironically then suffered another Final defeat, playing against his former Rovers in their shock RL Cup Final victory over favourites Hull in 1983.

To be a supreme specialist in the art of hooking would have been sufficient claim, but what made Bridges special was his extraordinary talent in loose play. He had great ball handling skills, was speedy in the loose, a fearless tackler and read the game well particularly from the acting half position. Such talent created many tries for his colleagues and he made a full and significant contribution to one of the finest Rovers sides in the history of the club.

Towards the end of the 1989/90 season, Leeds reserves were playing at Post Office Road and their young centre caused quite a stir amongst the meagre crowd as he cut through the Rovers defence for four tries in impressive style. This was duly noted by the Rovers officials and when money was available in the close season, following the transfer of Graham Steadman to Castleford, Leeds were approached and that young centre, Ikram Butt, was signed.

He was immediately thrust into the senior team and made his debut on 26 August 1990 at home to Bramley in the Yorkshire Cup. Rovers won 36-4 and Butt scored on his debut – but on the wing. Although he played the odd game at centre in his first two seasons, the Rovers rightly saw his main contribution to be on the wing.

Butt's main assets were his strength and his elusive running. In particular, his balance and powerful 'upper body strength' gave him the ability to bounce off players and twist and turn, almost on a sixpence (albeit old coinage!). He was a very busy player who would often come in off his wing to help the forwards before this tactic had become prevalent in the modern game. He had a roving commission to appear anywhere on the field, and this proved a very effective ploy.

In his second season, he scored 21 tries and played one of his finest games. On 28 September 1991, the Rovers were at Hull in the second round of the Yorkshire Cup and were losing 16-4. Two pieces of magic from Butt then brought them back from the dead in an incredible three-minute spell. He first collected the ball just inside the Hull half, bounced off three would-be-tacklers, and then beat two more defenders before sending Manning over from 10 yards. Three minutes later, he took the ball from Gary Price, side-stepped two defenders and rounded full-back Gay to score and level the scores at 16-16. Rovers won the replay at Featherstone 21-18 when Butt again scored. The crowds loved his punchy style and his best personal tally was four tries at home to Bramley on 18 April 1993, when Rovers won 78-0.

The Rovers were relegated to the Second Division in 1991/92, but they bounced back in convincing style in the 1992/93 season by finishing Second Division Champions and winning the Premiership Trophy against Workington at Old Trafford on 16 May 1993. He played his full part in these successes with his highest tally of appearances in a season (37) and 17 tries.

His ultimate accolade came on 1 February 1995 when he played for England *v*. Wales at Cardiff. Two months later, his other dream of a Wembley final evaporated at Elland Road in the RL Cup semi-final defeat by Leeds 39-22 (when he scored again). That was to be his last try for Rovers, as in the close season in May 1995 he was transferred to London Broncos – but what an impression he left at Featherstone. His example has since been utilised to encourage more ethnic Asians to play rugby league, and Ikram Butt is its prime motivator.

Total appearances: 168   Tries: 66   Points: 264

Richard Chapman
Hooker, 1997-present

There haven't been many goal-kicking hookers in rugby league and Richard Chapman, the present Rovers hooker, could claim to have had his goal-kicking prowess stifled! When he moved to Featherstone in 1997, the Rovers had two established goal kickers in Deryck Fox and Ty Fallins and his skills in this area were only required on an occasional basis. In 1998, with Fox departed, he vied with Fallins for goal-kicking duties and kicked 83 goals in 18 of his appearances. His best tally was nine goals and two tries at home to Leigh in Rovers 58-4 win in August. When Fallins departed, Jamie Rooney arrived on the scene and Richard has since concentrated on his other attributes – scoring tries and providing zip to the Rovers forwards!

Although born in Featherstone, Chapman's family moved to Dewsbury in the 1970s and it was from Dewsbury Moor that he signed for Sheffield Eagles in 1993 at the age of seventeen. He had limited opportunities there and declined a new three-year contract in 1996. After a brief spell at Dewsbury, he moved to Bordeaux in France to play rugby and after three months was told that David Ward the Rovers coach was interested in signing him. He arrived home the following day and signed! It was no surprise. His mother was a cheerleader for the Rovers in the 1970s and the family's Featherstone roots ran deep.

He made his senior debut *v.* Moldgreen in the RL Cup in January 1997 and he immediately fitted into the Rovers set-up. Although the number 9s in the present game do not have the hooking skills previously required, his lively and individual play, particularly from the acting half-back position, has endeared him to Rovers fans. His speed in loose play has led to his many tries and, having scored 81 by the end of June 2002, it is entirely possible that he will challenge the club try scoring record for a forward which is currently held by Peter Smith (110). Many consider his skills worthy of display in the Super League and he would dearly love to achieve that with the Rovers. Chapman came so close to that in 1998, when Rovers lost the

Division One Grand Final (and, with it, entry into the Super League) to Wakefield 24-22 in controversial circumstances. He gave an outstanding display, playing a major role in Rovers' first two tries and kicked three goals; he was deservedly named Man of the Match. Rovers were beaten in the closing stages after having a try by Pratt disallowed.

A tremendous club man, no-one will try harder to achieve Super League status for the Rovers than Richard Chapman. In these days of rapid player turnover, short contracts, and limited club loyalty, he has already enjoyed six seasons with Rovers and has turned down offers to move on. Always a crowd pleaser, he has the potential to achieve greater things at Featherstone.

Total appearances: 138 (+42) Tries: 81 Goals: 128 Drop goals: 2 Points: 582 (up to 30/06/02)

Mick Clamp

Wing/Centre/Second Row, 1952-60

Mick Clamp was a remarkably versatile player. He was equally at home in the centre or on the wing, scoring 55 tries in 114 games, and he then made the transition to second row forward and scored 35 tries in 96 games. He was born within sight of the Post Office Road ground, and his try scoring ability was evident for Featherstone juniors when he scored seven tries in each of four successive games.

Signed in 1952, he was deliberately groomed in the reserves and did not make his senior debut until August 1953 at York. Even with limited appearances his form was such as to gain selection for England Under 21s v.

France in April 1954. His first team career proper commenced in September 1954 and for almost three years he alternated as a centre and a winger with equal success. Weighing 14 stone and standing at 6ft 2in, he used his build to purposeful advantage and once moving at speed he was difficult to stop. In April 1957, it was decided to move him to the second row. He had scored 16 tries in a 17-game spell between 13 September and 26 December 1956, and one wondered how the transition would work. The answer was swift. He scored tries in the first two games and his power play became even more effective when operating in the forwards. He benefited from the well-timed passes of Fearnley and Lambert, and had exceptional speed to take full advantage of any space.

He continued his outstanding form, but injuries disrupted his progress. He missed five matches in December 1957 and returned to face Hull KR at home when he won the game almost single-handed. Seven matches later he fractured his hand at Keighley (when he scored two tries), an injury which caused him to miss the cup games against St Helens and Workington and probably cost him a place on the 1958 tour to Australasia. Undeterred, he resumed with his usual vigour and in another outstanding game v. Wigan in October, his powerful sorties were a feature and his try contributed to a 13-6 win. It brought him selection for a RL XIII against France in November. There were mixed emotions for Clamp in 1959 – disappointment that Hull prevented Rovers reaching Wembley after another great cup win over St Helens, but partial revenge when Rovers beat Hull in October in the Yorkshire Cup final.

On 19 April 1960, he played at Castleford in what was to be his last game. With his tally of injuries, he decided to retire from the game. This premature end to his career at the age of twenty-five deprived Rovers of an exciting player who could have gone on to greater things for both club and country. His attacking prowess and versatility made him a significant name in the history of the club.

Total appearances: 210   Tries: 80   Goals: 4   Points: 248

Terry Clawson

Second Row/Loose Forward, 1957-65 & 1978

Terry Clawson must rank as one of the most colourful and well-travelled characters in rugby league and when his remarkable career ended at Hull in 1980, he had concluded twenty-three years in the game. He scored 75 tries and 1,177 goals, made 640 appearances, played for nine different clubs as well as South Newcastle in Australia, had a Test career extending over twelve years and six months making 14 appearances, made 10 appearances for Yorkshire, played in seven Finals … and it all began at Featherstone!

Any youngster who could play for a county Under 17 side at sixteen and score 116 goals and 26 tries in one season, would appear to be special and Featherstone lost no time in signing him from their junior side in 1957. Indeed, he was one of a very talented trio signed from that side which included Malcolm Dixon and Roy Bell. His debut came on 28 December 1957 at home against Bramley in his accustomed position of loose forward. The following week, he was hooking against Tommy Harris, the Great Britain hooker at Hull, when Stan Moyser, the Rovers selected hooker, missed the train and Terry volunteered. The confidence of youth! He only made seven appearances that season and in the last one he fractured his leg at home to Halifax on 8 April 1958.

He resumed in 1958/59 when the absence of two Rovers stars gave him his opportunity. Cliff Lambert, the Rovers number 13, had to have a knee operation, Don Fox was also absent and Clawson took over the goal-kicking duties. He never looked back. From 1958 to 1963, he embarked on an incredible scoring sequence whilst at the same time emerging as a powerful and capable second row or loose forward. In his third season, he broke the club goal-scoring record of 102 previously held by Jack Fennell and Don Fox's points scoring record of 235, and two years later shattered his own record by kicking 125 goals and amassing 271 points. When he failed to score against Keighley in the Yorkshire Cup on 6 September 1960, it was the first time he had not scored since 4 May 1958, during which period he had scored 140 goals and 12 tries (316 points) in 41 appearances,

which works out as an average of eight points per game. On 6 March 1963, in Rovers' 32-2 home win over Batley, by coincidence both Don Fox and himself reached their 1,000th point for the club – Fox in 287 appearances, Clawson in an astonishing 160!

Such phenomenal form brought its recognition with the first of three county appearances in Rovers colours on 31 August 1960 and selection for Great Britain *v.* France in February and March 1962. At club level, he shared the delight of a Yorkshire Cup final victory over Hull in 1959, and the disappointment of the RL Cup runs which ended at the semi-final stage in 1959, 1960 and 1962. His best personal tally was 19 points (eight goals, one try), which he achieved twice, at home to Doncaster in November 1959 and at home to Bradford in August 1962. He kicked some wonderful goals and paved the way for victory in so many matches, but I particularly remember two visits to Workington in the space of one week in February 1959. Rovers

---

Total appearances: 216   Tries: 41   Goals: 487   Points: 1097

Terry Clawson in action against St Helens in the epic third round RL Cup encounter on 21 March 1959, when Rovers won 20-6. Cyril Woolford is assisting.

had never won at Derwent Park and in a league encounter there on 14 February, a try and two goals by nineteen-year-old Clawson featured in a historic first ever win by 10-0; a week later, four majestic goals by ice-cool Clawson secured an 8-5 first round RL Cup win. On 8 April 1963 at Widnes, he kicked a penalty goal from 10 yards within his own half. The touch judges disagreed on whether it had passed through the posts and the referee then ruled no goal. I and many others were convinced that it had gone over – and that was some kick!

After two matches at the opening of the 1963/64 season, he received the devastating news that he had contracted tuberculosis and was admitted to a sanatorium where he remained until March 1964. The club and players helped support him and his family during this traumatic time and fortunately he made a full recovery, returning to the senior team against Leeds in August, when he promptly popped over five goals. He was back,

but regrettably his Rovers career was soon to end. Despite all the success, he had made it known that he wanted to leave Featherstone. In January 1965 he was transferred to Bradford Northern for £3,000 and in 192 appearances he had registered 1,091 points (487 goals and 39 tries). That could have been the end but he returned for a further spell in 1978 and played another 24 games (this time as a prop), the last of which was away to Rochdale on 12 November 1978, when his son Neil made his debut for the Rovers.

Clawson contributed so much to the Featherstone scene. He was seemingly unflappable and fulfilled all his early promise. His goal-kicking was so dependable, and in play he was quick to learn with a maturity beyond his years, never shirking any forward tussles. His natural talent and ability obviously stood him in good stead and extended beyond his Featherstone years to forge what was an absorbing career.

Billy Clements
Second-Row Forward, 1921-28

Another of the elite thirteen who represented Featherstone in their opening fixture in senior rugby league at Bradford on 27 August 1921, Billy Clements had been a member of the all-conquering junior side of 1919 to 1921 and he quickly adapted to the senior game to play a vital part in Rovers' baptism in the 1920s. It was his 'excellent pass to Jimmy Williams' which led to Williams scoring Rovers' first try at Bradford. One week later, in the opening home game against Hull, Williams repaid the gesture: 'He broke from the scrum, Clements was in attendance to take his pass and force his way over the line with three Hull defenders clinging on.'

Although listed as a second row forward, Clements had a varied first season playing at prop, loose forward, hooker and centre as well as second row, but for the rest of his career it was predominantly second row, with the occasional move to the front row. He was very versatile and nimble considering his bulk. In his second season, he became the first Rovers player to gain county recognition when he played for Yorkshire v. Lancashire at Hull in December 1922. He made two other appearances for the County – in October 1923 at Hunslet, as hooker, when he scored a try and a goal in the 51-12 defeat of Cumberland, and at St Helens City in December 1925, when he was one of four Rovers players who helped secure a 26-10 victory over Lancashire.

For a forward, he was an adept try scorer and he had two tries in each of the games at home to Barrow in April 1922 and at home to Hull in February 1924. He was also a powerful goal kicker and he broke more than one window in the houses on Post Office Road. Luckily for the local homeowners, however, he was only used occasionally as Jim Denton and Jimmy Williams were the more regular kickers.

He was part of the pack which shook mighty Wigan in the epic second round RL Cup game in March 1923, when Wigan narrowly secured a 14-13 win. He also played in all three games of that incredible RL Cup first round encounter with Halifax in 1925. The Rovers travelled to Thrum Hall on 14 February and on a snow-covered pitch fought a tremendous duel at the end of which neither side had scored. The replay took place four days later in perfect conditions at Featherstone, when another tremendous forward tussle ensued. At half-time there was still no score, and even Billy Clements had been unsuccessful with his penalty attempts. A penalty goal to each side in the second half resulted in another drawn game 2-2, and so five days later, the second replay took place, this time at Headingley. Heavy rain preceded the game and after another absorbing encounter, Rovers finally won through 6-2. The games must have set up some records – 120 minutes were played before a score, and in the three games no tries were scored.

In the 1927/28 season, Clements was appointed captain, an indication of his popularity and the esteem with which he was held. It was therefore a surprise when, after leading his team to a hard fought 6-4 victory at home to Hunslet on 14 January 1928 as the Rovers strove for a top four place, he was transferred to Wakefield Trinity. This was yet another example of the Rovers having to sell one of their stars to ease their financial burden.

Total appearances: 176   Tries: 33   Goals: 12   Points: 123

Colin Clifft
Loose Forward, 1959-65

On 10 May 1956, Great Britain journeyed to France and were defeated by 23 points to 9 at Lyons. Rovers' Don Fox was scrum-half and playing alongside him at loose forward was a player whom neither realised would be resuming their partnership at club level four years later. That player was Colin Clifft, who was playing in Wakefield Trinity colours. He made 97 appearances for Trinity before joining Halifax in 1956/57 and it was from there that he joined Rovers in the exchange deal which took Alan Marchant to Halifax in November 1959.

He is one of the few players who played for his country before his county, and he was selected for Yorkshire on three occasions with Halifax. He made his Rovers debut at home to Doncaster on 28 November 1959, and within three minutes he had scored his first try. Initially, he played in the second row but after four games reverted to his original position, showing his capabilities to the full. At Castleford on Boxing Day, he was the complete master and tactician as he scored two great tries in Rovers 24-5 win. His style of play instantly suited the Rovers for with his long passes he could swiftly open up an attack and also dictate the plan of attack. The team was making a strong bid for League and Cup honours and at Thrum Hall in March 1960 he had the satisfaction of making the first try against his former colleagues which led to a magnificent 16-10 RL Cup victory. Unfortunately, he injured his shoulder the week before the RL Cup semi-final with Wakefield. His season was over and Rovers' hopes of honours disintegrated.

He returned at the beginning of the following season, 1960/61, but his shoulder was injured again v. Oldham in September. He resumed to provide a very effective back three permutation with Terry Clawson and Cliff Lambert as they rotated between second row and loose forward. He made 34 appearances that season and, despite an operation for appendicectomy in the close season of 1961, he continued to feature in what was a very successful Rovers team. In 1962, Wakefield again thwarted aspirations at the semi-final stage in both the RL Cup and League Championship play-offs. The following year saw Colin eventually make it to a final when the Rovers met another of his former clubs, Halifax in the Yorkshire Cup final. Sadly, the Rovers disappointed in losing a poor final by 10 points to nil, and Clifft broke a bone in his back which necessitated a support. He did not play again for the rest of that season. He was transfer-listed at £3,000 and both Huddersfield and Keighley made enquiries but he declared that he was staying at Featherstone, where both on and off the field he had never been happier. He was taken off the transfer list, stuck to his word and was content to play in the 'A' team. He played six games in the senior team at the beginning of 1964/65, his last match being at St Helens in October 1964, and he was then placed on the transfer list again at £1,000 but he chose to retire from the game. His constructive skills and adventurous approach had served the Rovers well, and it was a measure of his loyalty and regard for the club which ensured that he was happy to end his playing days there.

Total appearances: 117 (+1)   Tries: 14   Points: 42

Gary Cooper

Full-Back/Centre, 1958-66

When the Rovers signed Gary Cooper in 1958, his only taste of rugby league had been a short season with Featherstone juniors. In the opening game of the 1958/59 season, Jack Fennell the recognised full-back was injured and two days later Cooper was thrust into his senior debut at Bramley. It immediately became obvious that he was a stylish player with a fantastic turn of speed and the only criticism in those early days was his tendency to hang on to the ball. Yet his talent was evident. He made 33 appearances in that first season but strangely only scored one try that season, at home to Doncaster on 7 February 1959.

Cooper was in pole position at the start of 1959/60 and he got off to a blistering start. As if to erase the memory of a solitary try in the previous season, he dazzled with six tries in six games, including an impressive hat-trick in the 26-9 Yorkshire Cup victory against Hull KR. Then suddenly the sparkle went and after helping Rovers to a 14-7 win over Leeds in the semi-final, he asked the club not to select him as he was not satisfied with his own form. He was studying in London at the time, but did return to play five matches at the end of the season.

He only made 13 senior appearances in 1960/61 which included a brief flirtation at centre in two games. He was however, back at full-back in March in the controversial third round RL Cup tie at the Boulevard when Rovers hopes of a fourth successive semi-final were dashed with a debatable last minute try by Hull. The following week at Keighley he was at his most spectacular best, running 70 yards to score and then 60 yards to send Charlesworth in. The following season he decided to make a positive switch to centre, where his attacking style of play was even more pronounced and resulted in him scoring 18 tries – form which was enough for him to be selected for the 1962 tour of Australasia. He did not make the Test teams but scored 13 tries in 16 appearances.

The captaincy of the club was bestowed on him in August 1962 but he asked to be relieved in December as he considered his form was affected. It soon returned and the try he engineered for Waterworth at home to Oldham on 15 May 1963 was one of the best seen at Post Office Road.

Cooper had his differences with the club and asked to be transfer-listed for the second time in September 1963. The fee of £8,000 was the highest asked by the club, and his form seemed to justify the asking price. On 9 October in the Yorkshire Cup semi-final at home to Huddersfield, he tore a hole in the visitor's defence after 90 seconds, to send Jordan in for a try and 13 minutes later, side-stepped Haywood to put Lingard in and the game was won. He was then absent until December and upon his return was back in the full-back position, and for most of the rest of his Rovers career.

That career came to an end in September 1966, when he said he would not play again for the Rovers. His last game was at home to Batley in April 1966. He was then transferred to Wakefield Trinity for £3,000, where he enjoyed more success playing in both the Championship and RL Cup Finals of 1968. He was an unorthodox player but it was this which made him so elusive. He was deeply reflective about his game, could read play astutely and opponents struggled to contain him. It was once said that 'Cooper contributes class to every game'. There could be no better description nor tribute.

Total appearances: 187   Tries: 43   Goals: 9   Points: 147

Ray Cording
Winger/Stand-Off, 1950-55

An outstanding junior sprinter, Ray Cording was signed from the Featherstone junior team in May 1950 as one of the 'golden twins' [Keith Goulding, his centre, was the other], who had set the junior game alight with their exploits. With such a reputation, the Rovers had no hesitation in introducing him to senior football at home to Batley on 30 August 1950 at the tender age of eighteen. He soon opened his try-scoring account with his first at home to Barrow on 9 September.

The confidence was repaid as Cording soon developed into a promising winger and he hit the headlines with spectacular tries which confirmed his undoubted talent. In March 1951, he was selected to play for England Under 21s v. France, but he had to withdraw through injury. At Castleford on 17 March he 'took a blindside pass on his own 25 and beat man after man in a series of swerves and side-steps and then passed to Alan Tennant who had less than 10 yards to run and score'. In April he scored a great try at Dewsbury, 'using the touchline cleverly, he evaded Harry Street, Pollard and Thompson in a magnificent run'.

Allied to his pace he had a deceptive long loping stride and a devastating side-step off either foot, similar in style to the great St Helens winger, Stan McCormick. In January 1952, however, the Rovers were in a dilemma because of injuries and it was decided to put Cording in the stand-off position, partnering young Ray Evans. The Rovers lost 6-2 at Hunslet, but the half-back combination had worked. A month later, the RL Challenge Cup commenced and the partnership was to prove an effective component in a Rovers team which shocked and amazed the RL world with victories over Wigan and Leigh to reach their first ever Wembley final. Although defeated by Workington, the Rovers played their part in an entertaining game.

Evans and Cording were still the choice at the start of the 1952/53 season, but supporters were divided on which position Cording was best suited for. He performed well at stand-off, but did not have the acceleration associated with a number 6, whereas there was no doubt that his long striding style lent itself to the space afforded on the wing. In January 1953, he played his last game at stand-off and returned to the wing permanently. Unfortunately, he then dislocated his shoulder scoring against Doncaster and was out for the rest of the season.

Another scintillating 80-yard effort at Bradford at the opening of the 1953/54 season showed he was back in business and endorsed with six tries in the opening five games. The try-scoring then petered out with only eight in that season and seven in 1954/55. This was disappointing, but there was still a buzz when he got the ball. However, a knee injury sustained at Bramley on 14 September 1955 effectively ended his career. He had a cartilage operation and attempted to resume training two years later, but it was to no avail, and a promising career had come to a most disappointing end for player and supporters alike.

Total appearances: 140   Tries: 34   Goals: 10   Points: 122

Keith Cotton
Centre, 1961-73

Keith Cotton was signed from Featherstone Juniors at a time when the club was well endowed with centres – Ken Greatorex, Tony Lynch, Jim Hunt and Gary Cooper. As such, after making his senior debut at Halifax on 4 November 1961, he did not make another senior appearance that season. He did not fare much better the following season with only four appearances, but he persisted by learning his trade in the reserves.

His patience paid off and when Jim Hunt retired he took the offered chance in November 1964 and enjoyed the luxury of 20 consecutive matches to finish the season with 22 appearances. He remained in the starting line at the beginning of 1965/66 but with Gary Jordan operating in the centre and the arrival of Dave Hartley, he again struggled to maintain his place. Whilst it was acknowledged that his defence was exceptional, there were limitations in his attack. 1966/67 started like any other season with him drifting in and out of the senior team until coach Laurie Gant brought him back for the first round RL Cup tie at Bradford. Gant wanted the middle strengthening and Cotton responded in fine style. He played in all of the rounds in that magnificent run to Wembley and successfully bottled up the centre threat of the leading Yorkshire clubs Bradford, Wakefield, Castleford and Leeds. Indeed, he gained the reputation of being one of the few centres who could curb the phenomenal Neil Fox of Wakefield Trinity – one of the greatest centres.

Thus having missed out on a place in the Yorkshire Cup final against Hull KR earlier in the season, Keith trod the Wembley turf on that historic 13 May 1967 when the Rovers defeated Barrow by 17-12 to lift the RL Cup for the first time in their history. One of the decisive moments occurred early in the second half when Barrow, losing 9-7, were endeavouring to run the ball out of their own half. Ged Smith, their scrum-half, received the ball only to be crash-tackled by Cotton in very effective style. The force of the tackle was such that Smith lost the ball and

Vaughan Thomas, the Rovers winger, swooped in to gather and score a decisive try. That was Keith Cotton at his best.

Hopes of other medals depended on Rovers' appearances in the Yorkshire Cup finals of 1969 and 1970. Keith had maintained his place since the Wembley year, but did not play in the 1969 final and was in the team which lost to Leeds 23-7 in 1970. He enjoyed a testimonial in 1972 and received a then record cheque of £1,038 – proof of his popularity. He was on the fringe of the 1973 Wembley team, but after playing at home to Dewsbury on 1 May 1973 he moved to Batley. He then took to coaching and had two spells at Featherstone, in 1976/77 when the Rovers won the First Division Championship and in 1986 as assistant coach. Keith Cotton was whole-hearted in his approach to the game and never shirked anything despite the inevitable hard knocks which his renowned defensive work attracted. He was an excellent example of a player unstintingly working and developing his skills to their maximum – the backbone of any club.

Total appearances: 141 (+24)   Tries: 20   Points: 60

Paul Coventry was one of those players about whom fans were divided about which was his best position. There was no doubting that he was a talented footballer with a good pair of hands, side-step, swerve, speed and bravery which made him a good finisher – and a solid defence! But from his first season, the arguments raged and these continued for thirteen seasons. Signed from Fryston Juniors in 1970, Paul made an early entry on the senior stage playing as substitute at home to Hull on 19 September 1970 and Dewsbury (also at home) on 23 September, when he scored his first try. His first full match was, however, on 25 September 1970 at Salford (in the centre). In his first season he made nine appearances in the centre and three on the wing and in only his eighth appearance he was a substitute in the Yorkshire Cup final with Leeds on 21 November 1970.

From then the pattern varied as he alternated between wing and centre from season to season and he even threw in a few appearances at number 6 in the latter stages of his career.

Whichever position he played, he certainly gave pleasure and value for money. Naturally, he scored many tries and in his long career he had the satisfaction of scoring against most of the top wingers in the game. His best haul was four tries against Leigh (at home) in March 1974, and he scored a hat-trick of tries on four occasions, v. Keighley (at home) in October 1972, v. Leigh (away) in February 1977, v. Wakefield (at home) in April 1979 and v. Halifax (at home) in October 1980. His best season was 1972/73, when he scored 14 tries and at the end of which he played on the wing against Bradford in the Wembley Cup Final. He was all set to return the following year as the Rovers won through to another Wembley appearance against Warrington but a month before the final he broke his arm scoring against Salford.

That injury ruled him out of most of the 1974/75 season, and the following season, he reverted to centre and with 36 appearances, only missed three games. Injuries were prevalent in 1976/77, when he only made 17 appearances but he was able to share in the Rovers success as First Division Champions. Back on the wing in the following season, he had a barren period of tries for most of the season, but then scored six in the last four games.

There were disappointments in defeats in the Captain Morgan Trophy final v. Warrington in January 1974 (wing), and the Yorkshire Cup final v. Leeds in October 1976 (centre). He never gained representative honours but there are those who consider that if he had remained on the wing, he could have. He had the misfortune to break his arm again at York in October 1981, which meant an 11-month absence. During this time he was granted a testimonial. He returned to the senior team in September 1982 and after playing at Hull on 10 November (at centre), he was transferred to Wakefield for £10,000.

Irrespective of the position in which he played, Paul Coventry served the Rovers well both on and off the field. He is now a director of the club and is responsible for sponsorship and marketing – and, just as he did as a player, he is making a good job of it.

Total appearances: 286 (+15)   Tries: 86   Points: 258

Jim Denton
Winger, 1921-34

Jim Denton was without doubt one of the greatest players to don a Featherstone jersey and it must always be remembered that his achievements were gained in the crucial formative years of the Rovers as a senior club. As such, for half of the time that he played, the team was struggling near the bottom of the table with depletion of ranks as star players were sold to survive. The club can only be grateful that he remained for his whole career, although that was to be expected. The Dentons were a famous Featherstone sporting family – Jim and his brother Sid were stalwarts in the Rovers team through the 1920s and part of the 1930s and both, together with the other brothers Edgar and Raymond, were accomplished Yorkshire Council cricketers.

Jim only started playing rugby with the Featherstone junior team in 1918 at the age of 18. After one match in the reserves he was straight into the senior team which won eight cups from 1919 to 1921, a strong enough case for admission to the Northern Rugby League in June 1921. He was one of the historic thirteen who played the first senior game at Bradford on 27 August 1921 and kicked a goal in the 17-3 win. On 14 February 1934, he kicked his last goal for the club in the home game with Wigan. In that period he amassed 1,141 points (129 tries and 377 goals) in 440 appearances. He headed the points scoring lists in every season bar one from 1921 to 1934. The exception was 1928/29, when he was runner-up to Ben Gronow. His best seasonal tally was 17 tries and 36 games (123 points) in 1926/27, and his best match tally was 21 points (three tries and six goals) scored against Bramley in a 35-3 home win on 22 March 1933.

He never had any problems with acclimatisation to senior rugby league and whilst his main position was wing (and his partnership with centre Jack Hirst was one of the finest in the club history), he was versatile enough to play in most back positions. Indeed, one match report against Bramley when he reverted to full-back due to the late withdrawal of his brother Sid, commented that 'he only needs to go into the pack one of these days to have filled all positions'. He was fortunate in not having major injuries and made over 30 appearances in all but two of 13 seasons.

In such a lengthy career, he shared all the ups and downs of the club following its admission to senior status. When interviewed in the 1950s, his most outstanding memories were the historic RL Cup encounter with Wigan in March 1923 and the equally historic Cup encounter with Halifax in season 1924/25, when two replays were necessary before the Rovers finally won through to the second round. In all three games, no tries were scored and as the onus fell on the goal-kickers, he had the satisfaction of landing three of the four scored by the team. In the second replay at Leeds, he thwarted a late Halifax rally when he went down bravely on the ball before three Halifax forwards, and the ball burst and had to be replaced!

Total appearances: 440   Tries: 129   Goals: 377   Points: 1141

Jim Denton played in the famous RL Cup second round tie with Wigan in 1923 when Wigan were fortunate to win by 14-13. He and his team-mates were reunited and photographed before another equally famous RL Cup encounter with Wigan in 1952 when Rovers won 14-11. From left to right, back row: W. Williams, E. Barraclough, E. Richardson, T. Wynard, E. Woolley, A. Haigh, W. Clements, C. Hepworth, H. Goodall. Front row: Jim Denton, J. Hirst, W. Seymour, J. Williams, J. Kirkham, L. Mason.

He scored many memorable tries and goals, his best try possibly being the one scored in his personal best match tally of 21 points against Bramley in 1933 when he beat six defenders in a run from half-way. Many thought he should have been selected for the 1924 tour of Australasia, but he lost out to his nearest rival, Charlie Pollard of Wakefield, on the casting vote of the chairman of the Selection Committee. There was some compensation later that year when he made the first of four appearances for Yorkshire between 1924 and 1926. He captained Featherstone for two seasons.

It is a measure of his contribution to the club that the career records he created in tries, goals and points stood the test of time and were not, in fact, overtaken until the 1960s, when Jack Fennell initially passed his 377 goal record and Don Fox his 129 tries and 1,141 points records. His 440 appearances remains the one record which has not been broken and one imagines it will never be broken in today's fragmented game. Ernest Barraclough, who shared the same career period with him and retired at the same time, made 435 appearances but the only modern players to challenge him have been Peter Smith (419) and Keith Bell (417). Apart from Don Fox, only John Newlove has scored more tries. Records impress, but they do not necessarily convey to the reader the picture of a player who could on his day run through the opposition with ease, and who was renowned for his fierce but fair tackling. A natural footballer, it was his tenacity in both defence and attack which helped establish him as one the Rovers' truly great and loyal players.

Sid Denton
Full-Back, 1921-32

Of the many famous Featherstone families who have contributed to the Rovers cause, the most prominent would have to be the Dentons. Jim Denton was a legend in his own right, but his brother Sid, who played with him for most of his career, made his own mark in the history of the club. Both were members of the all-conquering Rovers junior team of 1919 to 1921 which was admitted to the senior league in 1921 and both played in the opening game at Bradford on 27 August – one on each wing.

Although playing all his football on the wing in that first season, Sid's true position was full-back and from the start of the 1922/23 season through to his retirement ten years later, he reigned supreme at number 1 for most of that period. He only missed four games in his second season, but one was the famous Cup-tie with Wigan. Yet Sid was to the fore in the famous first-round encounter with Halifax in 1925. Two drawn games at Halifax and Featherstone led to a further replay at Leeds where the Rovers finally triumphed 6-2. No tries were scored in any of the games and the reports highlighted Denton's 'fielding and kicking as well as his defence. Twice he saved certain tries with outstanding tackles' and in the third game it was reported that 'a feature was the kicking duel between Denton and Garforth which Denton won'.

There were many exploits to applaud from this stylish full-back. Two games against the mighty Huddersfield team when Sid's defensive stint helped the Rovers produce shocks were in October 1924, when Rovers won 7-4 at Fartown in the second round of the Yorkshire Cup, and at Featherstone in April 1929. In the latter game, Rovers were second from the bottom and Huddersfield were the league leaders. Sid was selected on the wing to give young Bill Warrington a chance at full-back. Playing out of their skins, the Rovers were hanging on to a 10-7 lead in the second half when 'Sid Denton was moved to full-back with Warrington under pressure and this proved a prime move because Denton had to repel Huddersfield attacks in the last twenty minutes using all his experience'.

Being the complete full-back, he had his moments in attack and scored 21 tries, the most famous of which was in April 1928 in the League Championship semi-final play-off at Leeds. With eleven minutes to go, the Rovers were hanging on to a surprising 10-7 lead when Leeds mounted another attack. 'Showing great anticipation, Sid Denton intercepted on his own 25, raced to half way, kicked, and beat Roberts the Leeds full-back to the bounce to score a great try under the posts'. Rovers eventually won to reach the championship final. Sadly, the Rovers were out of form as they lost 11-0 to Swinton and again in the Yorkshire Cup final against Leeds later that year 5-0. In that period, he had 59 consecutive appearances from 5 November 1927 to 26 January 1929, and from the beginning of the 1927/28 season to the end of the 1931/32 season he only missed six games playing in 198 of Rovers 206 games.

What a remarkable display of the consistency which was the hallmark of Sid Denton's career. He excelled in both attack and defence, playing his part in helping to establish the Rovers in the big league – and how he succeeded. He retired after playing at home to Hunslet on 17 September 1932.

Total appearances: 349   Tries: 28   Goals: 7   Points: 98

Malcolm Dixon

Prop Forward, 1957-70 & 1974-75

The story has been told many times, but when twelve-year-old Malcolm Dixon watched the Rovers lose at Wembley in 1952, he dreamed of returning as a player. Five years later, in 1957, he signed for the Rovers and that dream was fulfilled on 13 May 1967, when he captained the Rovers in their 17-12 win over Barrow to land the RL Cup for the first time in their history. All the early promise which Dixon had shown as a young player was also fulfilled and no-one deserved the honour more of receiving the cup from HM The Queen.

At 6ft 2in and almost 18 stone, Dixon was a colossus from his junior days. He was one of the famous trio of signings in 1957 from Rovers Under 17s side – Terry Clawson and Roy Bell were the others. He made his senior debut *v.* Dewsbury (at home) on 28 September 1957, but the club was content for him to learn his trade in the reserves, and after a handful of appearances in his first two seasons, he made his impact at the beginning

of the 1959/60 season. His mentors, Frank Moore and Joe Anderson, were both at Featherstone at this time, and passed on their vast experience for which Dixon was always grateful. He was included in the opening game at Halifax and turned in an outstanding display and never looked back. Within two months, and at the tender age of nineteen he had won a Yorkshire Cup medal as Rovers beat Hull 15-14. He never flinched as the Rovers embarked on one of their toughest RL Cup routes to the semi-final in 1960 with victories at Workington, Halifax and Swinton. At Halifax in the second round, a cauldron of a game, his touchline dash paved the way for the deciding try by Woolford which gave Rovers a 16-10 victory. In a 40-yard dash he made one of the best runs seen by a forward, as he showed exceptional speed and used his bulk effectively to brush Owen and Keith aside before handing to Woolford.

That was the essence of Dixon. Apart from being a powerful scrummager, he used his bulk powerfully with devastating bursts and his speed was exceptional for a big man. It meant, however, that he had more than his fair share of knocks and his career was disrupted by injuries.

After the initial success, he suffered the disappointments of defeat at the semi-final stage of the RL Cup in 1960 and 1962, and the Yorkshire Cup final defeats against Halifax in 1963 and Hull KR in 1966. By this time, he had taken over the captaincy following the departure of Don Fox to Wakefield and no-one could have envisaged what lay around the corner. Yet, inspired by Dixon, the Rovers added to their RL Cup feats by despatching the might of Yorkshire clubs, Bradford, Castleford, Wakefield and Leeds on their way to the 1967 final. Coach Laurie Gant and captain Dixon were an ideal combination and deserved credit for the way they led the team to such a historic victory.

He turned down a transfer to Wigan in September 1963 and his loyalty was rewarded with a testimonial in 1968 when he received a then record sum of £840. After another

---

Total appearances: 316 (+5)   Tries: 47   Goals: 41   Points: 223

Malcolm Dixon on the attack in the RL Cup semi-final with Wakefield at Odsal Stadium on 9 April 1960. Rovers lost 11-2, and this was the first of three semi-finals in which Dixon was involved. The third was more successful, as Dixon captained the Rovers to a 17-12 victory in 1967.

outstanding season as captain in 1969/70, he broke his ribs in the last game against Castleford. He returned against Dewsbury in September 1970, but this was to be his only appearance of the season. In 1972, having been released by Featherstone, he was approached by Gary Cooper, a former team-mate, to join York where he teamed up with Laurie Gant, and spent two very successful seasons; and even a re-call to the Yorkshire County side in September 1974 at the age of thirty-four. His vast experience benefited the young York side and, ironically, the Rovers turned to him again for that experience in November 1974 when he returned to Post Office Road. He played nine more games, his last being the RL Cup match with Salford (at home) on 9 February 1975. He returned to York in 1977/78 for a period as coach.

He made his international debut for Great Britain against France in February 1962 and made one more appearance, again v. France in March 1964. His solitary appearance for Yorkshire with the Rovers was v. Cumberland in September 1960. Certainly he had the talent and ability to have added more appearances, but injury did not help the cause. The fact that despite his crop of injuries he returned time and time again to grace the game for fifteen years speaks volumes for his commitment. His coach Laurie Gant summed him up as a cool, calm and very knowledgeable leader who could read a game and inspire others. He communicated with players and led by example. He was also a very good kicker of a ball, a talent he rarely used – all attributes which played their part in his success and that of the club in the 1960s. His loyalty and service to the Rovers continues to this day as he is a very active chairman of the Featherstone Rovers Past Players Association – and what a credit to the club.

Carl Dooler
Scrum-Half, 1960-69

Another Sharlston nursery half-back product was Carl Dooler. He joined Rovers in October 1960 and ironically he was later to oust another famous Sharlston product, Don Fox, from the scrum-half position. Carl made a confident debut *v*. Batley (at home) on 3 December 1960 and although he only made five appearances that season, his opening two tries against Wakefield (at home) in April 1961 showed his undoubted potential.

As understudy to Don Fox, his senior appearances were again limited in 1961/62 but he gained experience and his first medal with the victorious 'A' team who won the league Championship. In September 1962, with only 16 senior appearances to his name, he was thrust into the limelight with his selection for Yorkshire. Don Fox, the first choice, was injured, his deputy Keith Holliday's wife was ill, and the selectors took a gamble with this nineteen-year-old youngster. He took his chance in fine style, his display against Cumberland being described as 'exuberance and tenacity', and he was retained for the next game against Lancashire. Rovers now had a problem with two outstanding players competing for the number 7 slot. The situation was resolved a year later in September 1963, when Fox moved successfully into the loose forward position.

Dooler was now able to burst forth and fully develop his talents at scrum-half to fulfill that early promise. He reigned supreme until 1968, establishing himself as one of Rovers best scrum-halves. The 1965/66 season was a mixture. He set off in scintillating form, scoring four tries in an amazing 20-13 win at Widnes in October, and producing a brilliant display against Wakefield in the following week. However, in November he stayed away from training in protest against the club selling star forwards Ramshaw and Fox. Fortunately, he resumed in January and continued in the same vein of superlative form which earned him selection for the 1966 Tour of Australasia. There he played 15 matches and scored 5 tries. He was substitute in the Second Test *v*. New Zealand at Auckland and only the outstanding Tony Bishop prevented him from making his international debut.

There were more changing fortunes in the 1966/67 season. He gained further selection for Yorkshire against Cumberland and Lancashire in September and helped Rovers through to the Yorkshire Cup final *v*. Hull KR in October. His controversial dismissal in that game by referee Baker for alleged tripping caused uproar and certainly contributed to Rovers' defeat. He was later found not guilty by the RL Disciplinary Committee, which came as little comfort. The biggest prize came at the end of the season with the Rovers' victory at Wembley by 17 points to 12. Dooler's drop goal before half-time, and his break for Smales to score the decisive try, crowned an impressive display which earned him the Lance Todd Trophy as Man of the Match.

Scoring a try in Yorkshire's 15-14 win over the Australian touring team in October 1967, was indicative of his continued excellent form, but then in December in another dispute with the club he was transfer-listed at a record £15,000. After playing at Oldham on 24 August 1968, he stayed away. He was transferred to Hull KR in January 1969 for £6,500. As a scrum-half at Featherstone he was exemplary. His wholehearted enthusiasm, his superb service and breaks from the scrum, his industry in both defence and attack were all in the best traditions of Sharlston's famous scrum-halves who included Jonty Parkin, Herbert Goodfellow and Don Fox.

Total appearances: 199   Tries: 62   Goals: 15   Points: 216

Ray Evans
Scrum-Half, 1951-54

One of the most successful Featherstone intermediate sides was that of 1947/48, from which seven players were signed by the Rovers. Ray Evans was one of five of those players who made the transition to senior ranks after he was signed from the Under 19s in January 1951. He had the pedigree. He was the babe of the Evans family, two of whom (Wilf and Joe) had played for the Rovers in the 1930s. Wilf notched up 199 appearances, but it was the youngest brother who is possibly remembered more because of that famous 1952 RL Cup run.

When signed, Ray was coming to the end of his national service and was soon making his mark in the 'A' team. Early reports said that 'he showed much resource and defensive capabilities, but was prone to over-enthusiasm which put him offside'.

He made his senior debut v. Rochdale (at home) on 18 August 1951 after an impressive charity match outing against Castleford the week before. He scored in both games, but then lost his place temporarily to veteran Jimmy Russell when he had to report for 'Z' training. He was soon reinstated and as the 1952 RL Cup trail approached, the Rovers experimented with a new stand-off partner, Ray Cording, who had been switched from the wing. The partnership made its debut at Hunslet on 5 January and was an instant success.

Inspired by coach Eric Batten, Ray turned up for the Cup with three tries against Keighley and three weeks later, his two tries in an 8-7 win at Rochdale in the first round leg gave Rovers the advantage to embark on one of their most famous RL Cup runs. The thrilling victory over Wigan in the third round by 14 points to 11 exceeded all expectations and Ray played his part making the blindside scrum break to send Eric Batten over for his 400th career try and seal victory for the Rovers. In the semi-final against Leigh, Ray was denied a try when many thought he had scored, but Miller's goals put the Rovers through and Wembley beckoned. The Rovers lost to Workington by 18-10 but

were not disgraced, and Ray had the satisfaction of racing through to score his try just before the final whistle – his 11th in what had been a memorable first season.

Ray continued to star in the next season, but up and coming youngster Tommy Smales was beginning to threaten. If that wasn't enough, another promising youngster emerged at the beginning of 1953/54 season when Don Fox was signed. Ray managed to retain the scrum-half berth towards the end of the season, but competition was keen to say the least. He played in three of the opening four matches of the 1954/55 season but when Rochdale enquired of his availability, he was transferred there in September for £1,500. His last match for Rovers was on 23 August 1954 v. Widnes (at home).

Ray Evans was once described as a team's scrum-half in that he used his individual skills primarily for the benefit of the team. Although only of slight build, he was terrier-like in his play and had a distinctive 'crouch' style. Allied to his tenacity and quick acceleration, he was an important part of the Rovers team of the early 1950s which laid the foundation for further success.

Total appearances: 73   Tries: 21   Goals: 2   Points: 67

Steve Evans

Utility Back, 1976-82

Steve Evans was undoubtedly one of the most talented players ever to wear a Rovers jersey. After scoring 38 tries for Featherstone juniors in 1975/76, he signed at the end of that season. After a substitute appearance in September 1976, he made his full senior debut at Oldham on 12 December at centre, and while he shared the success of the First Division Championship, his appearances were restricted due to the form of Gilbert and Coventry, and he made only 12 appearances. He did, however, open his try scoring account with two at Barrow on 20 April 1977 which gave Rovers a 7-5 victory and sealed the Championship win.

Given his chance in the opening game of 1977/78, he went on to make 39 appearances appearing as centre, stand-off and wing – hence utility back. This ability to shine in various positions was a tribute to his natural flair and talent. His reputation as a prolific try-scorer was extended into senior football with 22 tries in that season. He scored two hat-tricks against Dewsbury (away) and Salford (at home). At Dewsbury, his second try was described thus:

'using his natural body swerve to full effect, side-stepped five defenders in a diagonal run for a glorious touchdown'. He had two more hat-tricks later in his career.

His outstanding form continued into the 1978/79 season, and at the end of the season he was named Young Player of the Year. Representative honours had to follow and they literally flowed from March 1979 to November 1980. He made his first appearance for England in March 1979 *v*. France (at stand-off), his full Great Britain debut in the Third Test *v*. Australia at Sydney in July (on the wing) and the first of four appearances for Yorkshire in August – and all this at nineteen years of age! Touring Australasia in 1979, he scored 16 tries in 19 appearances, including two in the Tests against New Zealand, and by January 1981 had made 13 appearances for Great Britain/England, including two at Under 24 level, when he captained the side.

In 1982, he created his own piece of RL history. On 2 February the Rovers played Hull KR in a preliminary round of the RL Challenge Cup following a decision to introduce professional clubs at that stage. Featherstone lost by 22 points to 18. Evans played in that game, but in the following week he was transferred to Hull for £70,000. He then went on to play for Hull through to the final and thus played for two clubs in the competition. Needless to say, the rules were changed to prevent it happening again. Evans made 166 appearances for Hull, sharing in their success and including an appearance at Wembley in 1983 against his former team-mates when Rovers upset the odds to win by 14-12.

There was no more thrilling sight than to see Steve Evans in full flow. A classy elegant player with pace, swerve and a brilliant side-step, he was at ease in any position, but most consider centre to have been his best position. It was unbelievable how he conjured up tries in unforgettable style. Some maintain that he should have made a world-beater with the talent he had. Be that as it may, he certainly graced the Featherstone scene and 76 tries in 140 appearances was an impressive legacy.

Total appearances: 131 (+9)   Tries: 76   Goals: 1   Points: 230

It is often said that one key ingredient of success in rugby league has to be a powerful pack. Featherstone had such a pack in the mid-1970s as they gradually dominated the First Division moving from 8th position in 1973/74 to the pinnacle of Champions in 1976/77. One particular component from 1975 to 1977 was the famous front-row trio of Jimmy Thompson, Keith Bridges and Vince Farrar. They first played together as a unit at Leigh on 28 September 1975 in a John Player Cup round and were to play 51 matches from then until the end of the 1976/77 season, when Jimmy Thompson was transferred to Bradford Northern.

For Vince Farrar, it was the culmination of ten years of persistence and patience and was typical of his determination to succeed, even though he was sorely tested on occasions. He signed for the club in March 1965 after trials as a hooker with the 'A' team. His first appearance was as substitute in the opening game of the 1965/66 season at Hunslet and his full debut came at Barrow on 28 August 1965. Yet it was not easy to establish himself in the hooking role. The Rovers had two veteran and experienced hookers in contention, Milan Kosanovic and Willis Fawley, but as they headed for retirement, young Graham Harris appeared on the scene in 1967 and in a meteoric rise he took the number 9 spot in his first season. He went from strength to strength in the following season, only missing two games. This meant few senior appearances for Farrar and when he played it was usually as a substitute forward. Tragically, Graham Harris's career was cut short through injury in 1968/69 and his misfortune gave Vince the chance he had been waiting for and which he took in great style. He played in all 40 league and cup games that season, a feat only previously achieved in peace-time football by two other players, also number 9s – Percy Morris and Joe Golby. Yet, in the first real acknowledgement of his versatility, he played eleven of those games at loose forward to help the club out of difficulties following the retirement of Tommy Smales.

It was in the number 13 jersey that he obtained his first medal when he played in the

1970 Yorkshire Cup final against Leeds – the first of three unsuccessful finals in that competition. His versatility was extended as he also played in the second row and, more significantly, at number 10, in the last four games of the season. From then on, this was to be his accepted position.

Another sound season in 1971/72 increased his stock and he added to his personal tally as substitute for Great Britain v. New Zealand in September (he was also a substitute in the Under 24 international with France in 1969);

Total appearances: 287 (+22)   Tries: 61   Points: 183

Vince Farrar scores in Rovers' 33-14 victory over Bradford Northern in the RL Cup Final at Wembley on 12 May 1973.

some consolation.

The Rovers were crowned First Division Champions at the end of season 1976/77, when Farrar's inspiring leadership and captaincy played a crucial role and earned him a nomination for the First Division Man of Steel Award (won by Malcolm Reilly). Six months later and it had all changed. The departure of Jimmy Thompson to Bradford was unsettling and whilst Farrar himself had the opportunity to join the Odsal club, he opted to join Hull and was transferred there in November for £10,000. His last match for Rovers was on 20 November at home v. Warrington. At Hull he enjoyed further success, captaining them through a record-breaking 26 wins out of 26 to take the Second Division Championship in 1978/79, and lifting the BBC Floodlit Trophy in 1979/80. He also played the last eight minutes of the 1980 RL Cup Final which Hull lost. He made that long awaited and coveted full appearance for Great Britain v. Australia (at the age of thirty-one) in the Third Test at Leeds, and added to his Yorkshire County record with two more substitute appearances. After retiring he joined the coaching staff at Hull, but then took the opportunity to coach at Featherstone from February 1981 to December 1982. He then played a season with the newly formed Sheffield Eagles in 1984/85 before finally calling it a day.

Farrar's achievements are inspirational. Through sheer dedication and perseverance, he reached the top of his profession and led the Rovers through their most successful period. What he lacked in physical stature, he more than compensated for with his solid down to earth and whole-hearted approach. He shirked nothing, was extremely powerful and played well above his weight; he also had the exceptional gift of making the half break and then making the ball available to his support. He was a great motivator, and justly deserved the then club record testimonial of £2,570 which he received in 1976. His record speaks for itself – and is not bad for someone who suffered from rheumatic fever as a child which threatened his future activity!

substitute then full appearance for Yorkshire in October; and 15 tries in 32 appearances for the Rovers. Later that year, the first of his knee problems occurred which kept him out of action for four months. He returned to play his part in the 1973 RL Cup run, scoring one of the tries in the 33-14 demolition of Bradford Northern in the Wembley Cup Final. But injury loomed again and, after only 10 appearances in 1973/74, he feared his career would be over when he suffered knee ligament damage. He was referred to the Durham specialist who had treated Jimmy Thompson, and was advised that there was a 50/50 change of a successful operation. He took the chance and although it meant that he missed the rest of the season, including the 1974 final, it was a success and he was able to take advantage of an offer to play for Cronulla (Sydney) during the close season of 1974.

He returned home in September and two further county appearances followed later that month, but then the season turned sour again when he had to have a cartilage operation. Undeterred, he returned to the fray when appointed captain and he was thus able to lead the Rovers in inspiring fashion through their glory seasons of 1975/76 and 1976/77. Hopes of another Wembley appearance were high in 1976, particularly after a stunning 33-7 third round victory over Leeds, but the Rovers then disappointed in losing the semi-final to Widnes. Finishing second in the league table came as

Willis Fawley
Hooker, 1950-67

When Featherstone Rovers played their first RL Cup Final at Wembley in 1952, the choice of hookers rested between veteran Bill Bradshaw and young Willis Fawley. Fawley had been signed in 1950 from the juniors but after a bright start, his form dipped and it was Bradshaw who got the nod. Fifteen years later, when the Rovers reached Wembley again, Willis Fawley travelled with the Cup squad in a gesture to acknowledge his Rovers career which had just ended after a record-breaking 16 years and 9 months – the previous record being that set by Frank Hemingway with 16 years.

His temporary lapse in form prior to Wembley 1952 was unfortunate because from taking over from Arthur Wood in 1951 to 1964 he was generally regarded as Rovers' premier hooker. He made his senior debut v. Keighley (away) on 10 March 1951 and scored his first try, v. Doncaster (at home), on 22 August 1951, the first of many tries to be scored by this very agile and speedy player. Indeed, during the 1950s, arguments raged as to who was the fastest hooker in the loose – Tommy Harris of Hull or Willis? Harris gained the representative honours which Fawley's form richly deserved but which never came. In encounters between the two clubs, their qualities seemed evenly balanced, particularly in 1959 when Hull beat Rovers in the RL Cup semi-final in April, but Featherstone were the victors in the Yorkshire Cup final later that year.

In the opening game of 1957/58, Fawley scored a hat-trick of tries against Leigh (at home), a feat he was to repeat against Keighley in September 1960. His try-scoring exploits reached their peak in 1959/60, when he set up a new club try-scoring record by a forward of 17 in one season. One of the most important tries he scored was in the epic third round RL Cup encounter at Swinton on 19 March 1960. Lambert's astute back pass was taken by Fawley to score under the posts and seal an incredible 11-7 victory over the powerful Lancashire side.

One of the most dramatic events was on Boxing Day 1954 in the derby clash with Castleford at Post Office Road. Half-way into the second half, Castleford were leading 6-3 and exerting pressure through a kick-through. Fawley chased back and in attempting to clear, stumbled and crashed heavily into the goal post. He was carried from the field on a stretcher and a gloom descended which was reflected in Rovers play. Ten minutes later, there was a tremendous cheer as Fawley re-appeared and promptly inspired Rovers to an 8-8 draw – yes, 'Boys Own' stuff!

He was certainly a hard player, but with his exceptional hooking skills and speed in the loose, he was also talented and very popular. He had a well-deserved testimonial season in 1960/61, when he only missed four games. The following season he was in the reserves, captaining them to the Yorkshire Senior Championship, and in November 1963 he out-hooked John Shaw, the reserve Test hooker, when he was brought back to play in the Yorkshire Cup final v. Halifax. He played the remainder of his games with the reserves and in a fitting gesture played one half of a final senior game v. Bramley (at home) on 5 April 1967, prior to Wembley at the age of 37 years 5 months. What a rousing reception he received, testimony to the esteem in which he was held.

Total appearances: 370 (+2)   Tries: 59   Goals: 9   Points: 195

Albert Fearnley

Second-Row Forward, 1956-58

Albert Fearnley was a member of the Halifax 'power pack' of the early 1950s and, as such, had achieved a great deal in rugby league when he arrived at Featherstone in September 1956. Two RL Cup Finals, three league Championship finals, two Yorkshire Cup finals and six appearances for Yorkshire were indicative of the team and the person. He had a reputation as a strong, robust forward and many queried Featherstone's decision to buy him.

Rovers had started the 1956/57 season with four successive league defeats and, ironically, Fearnley's debut was against the team which he had left a few days earlier. In a story book beginning, he inspired the Rovers to a shock 22-9 victory over Halifax, 'did much to solidify the Rovers pack', kick-started the Rovers' league programme and won over the Post Office Road fans. As a Rovers' colleague of the day recalled, he brought fire to the pack at a time when the team needed backbone. Two months later, he inspired another famous victory – this time over St Helens at Featherstone. He supported Lambert to score the first try and then sealed a 15-6 win with a powerful surge to score again – making it 5 tries in only 10 games. No wonder he was appointed captain shortly after his arrival.

Coach Bill Hudson resigned in March 1957 and the club did not advertise for a successor, but asked Albert to coach the forwards. This he agreed to, but in April he asked to be relieved of the responsibility as he considered he could not give his best as a player. This was typical of the man – he had to give 100 per cent to his task.

Nine tries in 27 appearances as a thirty-two year old was a creditable first season, but he improved on this in 1957/58. He only missed four matches out of 44 league and cup games as Rovers strove for league and cup honours. The 1958 RL Cup campaign was notable for the memorable victories against Barrow in the second round and St Helens in the third round. In a titanic struggle with the Barrow pack, the Rovers forwards were magnificent, led by Fearnley. He collapsed with exhaustion in the dressing room after the game but there were more heroics to follow as the Rovers battled to defeat St Helens in a snowstorm in a memorable 5-0 win. Again, Fearnley played his part and it was all so disappointing that these efforts could not have been rewarded with a Wembley visit, but Workington dashed the hopes in the semi-final. On a personal note, he was delighted with his season's tally (notching another nine tries) and an aggregate of 52 appearances out of 62 games in just under two seasons. It was Featherstone's loss when sadly he was in dispute with the committee during the close season and left to join Batley as player-coach – and immediately plotted Rovers downfall in the first round of the 1958 Yorkshire Cup.

Players and supporters alike responded to Albert's whole-hearted approach to the game. Extremely fit, he played a full 80 minutes, always in the thick of it, and was always highly competitive and inspirational. He set the example by foraging and tackling to a high degree, encouraging his colleagues and inspiring them to their full potential. What an impact! He devoted his life to rugby league and the Rovers were extremely fortunate that part of that career enlivened the Featherstone scene.

Total appearances: 67   Tries: 18   Goals: 2   Points: 58

Jack Fennell
Utility Back, 1952-65

The term 'utility back' was probably invented for Jack Fennell, who was one of the most versatile players ever to play for the club. He was signed as stand-off, made his name as a full-back with 273 appearances and he also had spells both in the centre and in wing positions. He did not appear as scrum-half, but no doubt he could have coped. Put simply, he was such a natural footballer that he could have made a success of any position.

Signed in December 1952 from Bagleys Rec's, he made an early senior debut at stand-off on 20 December at home to York and he kicked his first goal in the return encounter at York a week later. Instant success did not follow, particularly when Joe Mullaney was signed in June 1953 and proceeded to play 36 consecutive matches before being injured at Easter 1954. Fennell deputised for him in the last three matches. His versatility emerged in the following season as he played in four different back positions. Sometimes, however, one can be too versatile and for Jack there was now a need to establish himself in one position other than stand-off. He had had his first outing at full-back at Workington on 21 August 1954 and when he had an early opportunity at the beginning of season 1955/56 to move from wing to full-back, he took it.

From then to the beginning of 1964, he occupied the number 1 spot, his only serious challenger being Gary Cooper, whose distinctive attacking flair from full-back was in contrast to Jack's solid and dependable approach. He lost his place to Cooper from 1958 to 1959 (and, typical of the man, continued to pass on his experience to Cooper). Cooper then switched to centre, where his style was even more prominent but allowed Jack to resume. However, when Cooper reverted to full-back early in 1964, Fennell's senior career was effectively over. He made six appearances in 1964/65, but then called it a day.

Nevertheless, he rewrote the record books during his long stay at the top, and made an immediate start in 1955/56 when he enjoyed his first full season, appearing in 40 of the 41 matches played. In schoolboy and junior football, he had been a prolific goal kicker and

resuming those responsibilities with the seniors, he became only the second Rovers player to kick a century of goals. In the last home game of the season he kicked three goals to reach his century and with 102 goals, broke the club record of 101 set up by the legendary Freddie Miller. He also topped the first 'Player of the Season' award. Two seasons later, he amassed another century and with 101 goals and four matches left, he was injured at Wakefield which deprived him of extending his record. Another injury at home to Castleford on Boxing Day 1956 halted a record run of 63 consecutive appearances.

He took part in the epic Rugby League Cup campaigns to the semi-finals in 1958, 1960 and 1962, and was also full-back in Rover's first ever Yorkshire Cup final victory in 1959, when Hull were beaten 15-14. In 1962/63, he was awarded a testimonial and responded by playing some of his best football in an outstanding season. Although Clawson and Fox had taken over the main goal-kicking duties, he added another 42 to his tally and had played in 39 consecutive matches when he was injured at Widnes with five matches remaining.

Total appearances: 320 (+3)   Tries: 30   Goals: 455   Points: 1000

Jack Fennell, the last line in defence in Rovers' 9-0 defeat by Wakefield Trinity in another RL Cup semi-final at Odsal Stadium on 11 April 1962.

Many tributes were paid to Fennell, but the most apt appeared in his testimonial programme as follows: 'I have seen Fennell agitated on the football field, but never lose his temper. He has been out of touch but never stopped trying. He has been one of an outclassed team, but has never despaired. It always seemed that a Featherstone jersey compelled him to give of his best. His greatest attribute was a virtue common to all outstanding ball players – his timing. It had to compensate for a lack of inches, a lack of pounds and a comparative lack of pace against fliers, but it seldom failed to make up for all three. How else does he halt the heaviest forward, break through the thickest ruck and stand as a model to all aspiring goal-kickers? Nor is it without significance that Fennell won back the first-team position from which he was dislodged. Not only did he win it back, but he held it with constantly growing conviction. It all ties up with the characteristics of persistence, courage and modesty which made him such an outstanding club man.'

He was the supreme utility back. His tackling and positioning were superb and his tackling technique in which he wrapped himself around an opponent, large or small, was amazing. He played and won so many matches for the Rovers and a favourite is the third round RL Cup-tie at Leigh in March 1955. Fennell was a last-minute replacement at stand-off for the injured Joe Mullaney. In a hard fought game littered with penalties, defences dominated and in the first half both Ledgard and Don Fox missed penalty goal attempts. Captain Ken Welburn turned to Fennell, who slotted his first goal over before the interval and following with two more in the second half. With 10 minutes remaining, Rovers led 11-9 and Leigh threw everything into attack. In a white hot atmosphere, another penalty was awarded to Featherstone in the closing stages and, showing the coolness of a veteran, Jack kicked his fourth goal from four attempts and the game was won. In another thrilling game v. Wigan (at home) in September 1955, Rovers were leading 6-3 but under pressure. Within the space of a few minutes, Fennell made two incredible weaving runs through a mesmerised defence and then popped up in the corner to carry Bolton out when a try seemed certain – moments which inspired a 13-6 win.

In his remarkable career, Fennell was described as the 'best full-back never to play for Yorkshire', but his exploits for the Rovers earned him such a special place. He scored exactly 1,000 points, his best tally being 19 points (one try and eight goals) v. Hull KR (at home) in Rovers' 46-5 Yorkshire Cup win over Hull KR on 31 August 1957. His last game was at Batley on 10 April 1965.

Deryck Fox
Scrum-Half, 1983-92 & 1995-97

On his first sight of Deryck Fox, who had signed for the club from St John Fisher, Dewsbury in August 1983, Rovers coach Keith Goulding said: 'Only seen the lad in training, but you can smell 'em. Has pace, ability and a very good pair of hands, and undoubtedly a star of the future.' It did not take long for the prophecy to come true. In his first professional game with the reserves, he kicked four goals, one drop goal and set up the two tries scored. He was immediately drafted on to the senior team sheet and, after two substitute appearances, made his full debut *v.* Whitehaven (away) on 18 September 1983. Another sparkling display earned him the first of many Man of the Match awards and his team their first victory of the season. He had arrived and the fans were set to enjoy what was to be a remarkable run of consistency by the young starlet. In the return game with Whitehaven two months later, he weighed in with two tries and eight goals (24 points) and yet while he was a very capable goal-kicker, he did not get many opportunities in his earlier years with Steve Quinn and Graham Steadman around.

Yet no-one was able to oust him from the number 7 spot and from 1983 until the end of 1991/92, he played in 309 of the 322 games played by the club – an average of almost 35 appearances per season. In this remarkable record, he made 60 consecutive appearances from 14 February 1988 to 7 November 1989. Representative honours had to follow and, again, his consistency shone through. The call came from his country first when he played for the Great Britain Under 21 side *v.* France in December 1984 and his full senior debut was *v.* France at Leeds on 1 March 1985. He won the Man of the Match award with two tries and one goal in the 50-4 victory and made nine successive appearances before losing his place to Andy Gregory in November 1986. From 1989 to 1992, he made four substitute appearances. He also toured Australasia with Great Britain in 1990 and 1992. On the county scene, his Yorkshire debut was against Lancashire on 11 September 1985 – the start

of a run of eight consecutive appearances until September 1991.

On the club front, the Rovers were in a constant battle for survival in the First Division and were eventually relegated to the Second Division in 1987. Deryck was a model of consistency as he led Rovers back into the First Division at the first attempt, but there was disappointment at the 28-26 Premiership Trophy defeat to Oldham in May 1988. Yet in spite of his 100 per cent effort and endeavour, he thought he could better himself with another club. The seeds were sown in 1986 after he had spent a summer with Western Suburbs in Australia, from where he submitted a transfer request which he later withdrew. The Rovers were thankful that he renewed further contracts, but when Rovers were again relegated to the Second Division in 1992 (despite his first century of goals – 109), the writing was on the wall. He returned from the 1992 tour of Australasia and Papua New Guinea, where he had captained the mid-week side, declaring that he wanted to

Total appearances: 351 (+3) Tries: 84 Goals: 373 Drop goals: 63 Points: 1145

Deryck Fox adds his contribution to Rovers' record Yorkshire Cup win over Keighley by 86-18 on 17 September 1989.

move, despite being in contract, and he did not resume training. He was reluctantly transfer-listed by the club and was transferred to Bradford in September 1992 for £140,000 – a then club record.

He returned to the fold from Bradford in November 1995 after yet another model of consistency. He made 107 appearances in just over three seasons, scoring 744 points (with centuries of goals in 1993/94 (131) and 1994/95 (123). Predictably, he starred in his opening return game, inspiring a 34-18 victory over Hull on 20 November 1995. He made 45 appearances before transferring to Batley after his last game for the Rovers *v.* Wakefield (away) on 8 June 1997, after a flurry of 46 goals in 13 matches. A year later, he reappeared at Post Office Road as player-coach to Rochdale and, typically, kicked seven out of eight goals and set up half of the tries as his team won 48-18!

Featherstone's knack of producing top-class

scrum-halves is legendary and Deryck Fox was another out of the top drawer. His consistency has been the underlying theme of this profile and has been bettered by very few players. In his Rovers career he was only substituted in 3 of 354 games and with Bradford once in 107 games – a total of only 4 in 461 games! He was utterly dedicated in his commitment and with his scurrying darting runs he had defences guessing most of the time. His kicking game was superb as he developed the art of the 'up and under' and switch kick to devastating effect. Apart from his own points-scoring, his scintillating and productive play created so many tries for his colleagues – and, of course, he had a particular liking for drop goals (63). To win the John Jepson Player of the Year Award on three occasions was a rare achievement and to retire finally from the game with a total career record of 1,982 points (109 tries, 733 goals, 80 drop goals) in 506 matches confirms Keith Goulding's assessment.

Don Fox

Scrum-Half/Loose Forward, 1953-65

One normally envisages a scrum-half of considerably smaller stature than 5ft 9in and 13st 3 lb, but those were the physical attributes the Rovers acquired when they signed seventeen-year-old Don Fox in 1953 from their junior side. These were unconventional attributes for this position at the time, and caused some contemporary debate, but Fox answered the sceptics in a compelling and direct manner. He was a brilliant footballer and achieved the most prolific points-scoring feats for the club, the like of which had not been seen since the days of Jim Denton in the 1920s.

He made his senior debut *v*. Leeds (away) in the second leg of a Yorkshire Cup game on 9 September 1953. Tony Allen was the goal-kicker then and it was not until his third match, at Rochdale on 19 September, that Fox kicked his first goals – three which won the match 9-6. In the next match, *v*. Hull, the Post Office crowd was treated to 14 points (2 tries, 4 goals) in a 29-7 win over Hull and he followed this up with all 13 points in a drawn game with Keighley, levelling the scores with a last-minute penalty. The points avalanche had begun, with extraordinary talent and maturity from a seventeen year old.

The Fox machine then just went on and on. He had his competitors who challenged, but the departure of such talented scrum-halves as Ray Evans, Tommy Smales and Alan Marchant to other clubs was testimony to his unrivalled performances. When yet another talent was unearthed in Carl Dooler (another Sharlston product), it was decided to absorb both of their abilities by switching Fox to loose-forward *v*. Leeds (at home) in the second round of the Yorkshire Cup on 17 September 1963. Such was his talent that he was equally at home in this new position and, after only six appearances, he played for Great Britain against Australia in the number 13 jersey at Leeds on 30 November 1963, scoring a try and playing a prominent part in Great Britain's face-saving 16-5 victory.

What a season that was for Fox! He shared a joint testimonial with his long-standing half-

back partner, Joe Mullaney, was captain, and set up more records. Initially, he had set up a new seasonal points record of 235 points (19 tries, 89 goals) in only his second season (1954/55), but this was then broken by Terry Clawson in 1959/60 with 256. Undeterred, Fox regained the record in this amazing 1963/64 season with his first century of goals (129) – another record – and 294 points in 40 appearances. He had a personal and club match best of 12 goals and one try (27 points) in the cup game *v*. Stanningley and for good measure broke the all-time club record of most career points when he overtook Jim Denton's 1141 points *v*. Wigan (at home) on 14 December 1963. No wonder he was the Player of the Season.

With such a phenomenal record, it is difficult to single out any of his outstanding performances. His goal-kicking won many matches, but in scoring more tries than any other Rovers player (162), there were many games to choose from. No other scrum-half

---

Total appearances: 368 (+1)   Tries: 162   Goals: 503   Points: 1492

Don Fox scoring one of his record 162 tries in Rovers' 15-11 win against Castleford on 27 October 1962.

could have scored the try literally through the scrum against Hull in the Yorkshire Cup final in 1959 which set the Rovers on their way to victory, and while he used his bulk on that ploy many times to score, his talent created others. Against Halifax in September 1956, he ran 60 yards, beating four defenders, to register an amazing score. Against Hunslet in January 1957, the visitors were leading 9-4 with 12 minutes to go. In a grandstand finish, he created a try for Fennell, converted the try from the touchline and won the game with a dropped goal three minutes from time – just two more snippets of a magisterial footballer.

He made his full Great Britain debut *v.* France at Bradford on 10 April 1956, scoring two tries in the first of three appearances. His county debut followed his country debut on 19 September 1956, again the first of three appearances for Yorkshire. He toured Australia in 1962, but had to return through injury after only five appearances and missed the New Zealand part of the tour. In September 1965, he was transferred to Wakefield Trinity for £3,000 and there he made up for his previous disappointments of missing out at the semi-final stage of the RL Cup in 1955, 1960 and 1962 by playing at Wembley in 1968. Trinity lost to Leeds 11-10 in that dramatic 'water-final', but Fox justly won the Lance Todd Trophy as Man of the Match.

His natural footballing ability, his powerful short dashes near the line, his accurate kicking and his perfectly executed moves were all sheer delight for those who had the privilege of watching him, and they were all the trademark of a remarkable player. At one stage he held every club record bar one until the equally remarkable Steve Quinn eventually came along to take most of them. Nevertheless, thirty-five years after his departure, in the club annals he has scored most tries (162), is second in points scoring with 1,492, third in goal-kicking with 503 and eighth in appearances with 369: a truly great player by the highest standards.

Laurie Gant
Utility forward, 1948-53

When Laurie Gant joined the Rovers in March 1948 from Wakefield Trinity, the team was languishing near the bottom of the league and had lost twenty-one matches on the trot. He was signed to provide experience and made his debut against Huddersfield on 28 March. It did not stop the rot immediately but a week later, victory by 12-8 at Hull KR was greeted with acclaim. Apart from ending an unenviable record of twenty-three consecutive defeats, it gave the players their first bonus which had been offered since Christmas.

It was in the following season that he made his mark (in 31 appearances). The Rovers pack at that time was young and raw, and from the outset Gant's experience provided the framework for the younger players to feed off and learn from. He was a natural leader who gave 100 per cent and when Freddie Miller and Eric Batten arrived, the experience was moulded into an effective combination.

The culmination of this was 1952, when the Rovers reached Wembley for the first time with historic wins over Wigan and Leigh. He was the driving force of the pack and never more so than in the semi-final game with Leigh. He literally left his sick bed to play on that bleak Saturday afternoon and what a sight it was to see him matching the might of the very talented Leigh pack. He was dubbed a 'pocket Hercules' after that game, but that had been the tag given to him by Rovers fans since he arrived. What he lacked in inches (5ft 7.5in and 14st 9lb), he compensated for with a bulky frame and an indomitable spirit.

He headed the club try-scoring list in 1950/51 with eight tries (the team finished third from bottom) and the one scored at Huddersfield prompted this report – 'a typical bulldozing effort which makes supporters wish that he could infuse some of his swashbuckling directness in his colleagues'. He played in every position in the pack, but was best placed in the second row. It came as a surprise when he was transferred to Hunslet in October 1952 after playing what was his last match for Rovers against the Australian touring team on 1 October 1952.

He retired from active football in 1954 and then had successful careers in refereeing and coaching, both as rugby league national coach and at club level. His appointment as coach at Featherstone in 1966 was the prelude to another return to Wembley as he masterminded an average Rovers side to unlikely but decisive victories over the top Yorkshire clubs Bradford, Wakefield, Castleford and Leeds to reach the RL Cup Final in 1967. Full credit was given for his part in bringing the Cup back to Featherstone for the first time, which compensated for the disappointment of 1952. He resigned as coach in 1970 and is one of the eight remaining members of the 1952 Wembley side.

He was awarded the MBE for his services to rugby league in 1981, and was mentioned in dispatches for his valour in the D-Day landings in 1944. Some player, some man.

Total appearances: 112   Tries: 15   Goals: 1   Points: 47

When one looks back on the career of Mick Gibbins, one can only admire what he achieved despite set-backs to which lesser players would have succumbed. He did not find it easy to break into the senior team initially and, when established, injuries cropped up at vital times. A mysterious back injury severely disrupted his career from 1978 to 1981 at a time when he had been playing his best football. In spite of this he battled on and regained his place in time to play his part in the 1983 RL Cup win over Hull at Wembley. He qualified for a testimonial and eventually completed sixteen seasons with the Rovers. His greatest asset was described as his determination to succeed and this was certainly reflected throughout his career.

Signed from Featherstone juniors in December 1970, he spent the best part of his early years in the reserves. He made his senior debut v. Rochdale (away) in September 1971 but, with the Rovers power pack of the 1970s,

he found himself mainly on the fringe and it was not until that pack was broken up after the First Division title win in 1977 that he was able to command a regular place. His form was such as to gain him Great Britain Under 24 honours against France in 1977. Typical of his displays was that in the RL Cup semi-final v. Leeds in April 1978 when, despite a Rovers defeat, it was reported that 'prop Gibbins was the mightiest forward on view'.

In 1978 he was struck with a mystery back injury which plagued him for three years. Yet he doggedly persisted in trying to pursue his career despite the injury and there was partial recompense in his selection for Yorkshire's two games in 1979, even though he only managed thirteen club appearances that season. Fortunately, he won through when the injury subsided in 1981 and he celebrated with one of his best seasons in 1981/82 with 31 appearances, 5 tries and the Player of the Year award. A testimonial followed in 1982/83, crowned with an appearance at Wembley as he played his part in the RL Cup win over Hull.

Peter Fox, who coached him twice at Featherstone, described him as 'a first-class grafting forward, tenacious, fearless, a complete text-book tackler who played to the best of his ability at all times – a coach's jewel'. His exceptional defence was particularly remarkable for a second-row forward who 'progressed' to prop. One of many outstanding games was the third round RL Cup-tie with Leeds in March 1976 when Rovers produced an amazing 33-7 win. Gibbins' performance was described thus, 'He tore into the defence with fervour and his late try was a reward for a great all-round game'.

In 1986, he played in the opening two games of the new season and after playing at Leeds on 3 September he was transferred to Hull the following week.

Gibbins showed great character and determination which enabled him to overcome a career-threatening back injury and re-establish his fitness and career to become a successful and respected professional.

Total appearances: 280 (+51)   Tries: 12   Points: 36

John Gilbert
Winger/Centre, 1976-86 & 1987

John Gilbert burst upon the Rovers scene in January 1977 after signing from Jubilee juniors in 1976. In his first senior appearance, he came on as a substitute *v.* Wakefield (at home) and scored a try, and a week later in his full debut he scored two tries, one after an 80-yard dash – and at Wigan into the bargain! Ten tries in 16 appearances was not a bad return for his first season and his impact made many forecast a glittering career. He was phenomenally fast and elusive, could read a game and was extremely powerful – a natural, and the type of player who made the crowds buzz with expectancy when he got the ball.

The Rovers benefited from these qualities. In seven seasons he was a permanent fixture, mainly in the centre, although he did make 53 appearances on the wing. After playing his part in the First Division Championship in his first season, he had to be satisfied with a runners-up medal in the Yorkshire Cup final against Castleford later in 1977. He had one of his best seasons in 1979/80, being ever-present with 31 appearances and hitting his highest try tally of 16. One of his outstanding games was the third round RL Cup-tie at St Helens on 12 March 1983, when he sliced through the St Helens defence to score two tries to help the Rovers to a surprise but convincing 11-10 victory. This set up the eventual equally surprising win over Hull in the final.

Six months later, it all changed for Gilbert, and upon his return to St Helens in November, ironically at the scene of one of his greatest triumphs, he sustained a cracked knee-cap which put him out of action for the rest of the season. He returned for 1984/85, making 27 appearances and registering his first hat-trick of tries against Bradford (at home), [he had scored two tries on 15 occasions during his career]. In November 1985 he asked to be transfer-listed and moved to Widnes in February 1986. He never gave the impression of really being settled at Widnes, making only 23 appearances and scoring five tries. In October 1987 he returned to Featherstone on a match by match loan basis, but only played three games, his last match being *v.* Castleford (at home) on 15 November 1987.

His talent was unmistakable and was rewarded with three appearances for the Great Britain Under 24 side *v.* France (home and away) in 1977, and in France in 1981. Many thought that such talent could have achieved more in the game, but he achieved much for Featherstone.

Total appearances: 240 (+3)   Tries: 80   Points: 253

Although he was born in Streethouse in 1908 and played for Streethouse Red House juniors, Joe Golby's route to Post Office Road took thirty years and followed stalwart service with Dewsbury and Wigan, two of the top clubs of the 1930s. At Dewsbury he was one of a renowned front row of Banks, Golby and Taggart, who were all eventually transferred to Wigan and played in the 1934 Championship play-offs final when Wigan beat Salford 15-3. Golby made nearly 200 appearances for Wigan and played in every game in one season. A specialist hooker, he was transferred from Wigan in exchange for the Rovers hooker, Vic Darlison. He made his senior debut on 15 October 1938 v. St Helens Recs (away), but it was reported that he 'was then transfer-listed at his own request in January after having given Rovers abundant possession since moving from Wigan last October'. Rovers immediately signed hooker Bowden from York, but he had a long wait ahead of him as Golby continued to play. It is not clear whether he withdrew his request.

In a remarkable sequence, repeating his Wigan record, Golby made 69 consecutive appearances in league and cup games from his debut in October 1938 to June 1940. Then having reached the Yorkshire Cup final v. Wakefield at Odsal, he was dismissed from the field together with his opposing hooker – one Vic Darlison, who was now guesting for Wakefield. He had the satisfaction of receiving a winner's medal, but the resultant suspension meant that he missed the opening two games of season 1940/41 (when Bowden at last took over). He then continued with his remarkable sequence and added another 29 as the consistency continued; indeed, at the end of his Rovers career, he had played in 118 of 127 games in a four-year period.

He was appointed captain in March 1942, but was powerless to avoid Rovers' heaviest ever defeat on 14 April 1942 at Halifax by 70-2. There were extenuating circumstances. The Rovers lost three men through injury before the interval and lost another after 60 minutes, playing the last 20 minutes with nine men. Golby played six matches in 1942/43 before being transferred to Batley, where he ended his career. His last match for the Rovers was at Hull in the Yorkshire Cup on 24 October 1942, thus concluding an impressive record. A true professional, his experience and skill helped blend a young Rovers side to forget the dismal record of the 1930s and win their first trophy.

Joe Golby was a fine footballer, with a compelling dummy and a strong presence at the acting half position. More importantly, he was an outstanding striker in the scrum, one of the best of his era, at a time when this provided the major source of possession. His competitiveness and professional pride were intense – he was only dismissed twice in his career and on both occasions he was opposed by Darlison.

Total appearances: 118   Tries: 5   Points: 15

Jeff Grayshon
Prop Forward, 1988-91

When coach Peter Fox signed veteran Jeff Grayshon from Bradford in August 1988, eyebrows were raised. Admittedly Grayshon had won every honour in the game (except a Wembley appearance), which included 13 Tests for Great Britain [he holds the record of the oldest player to play in a Test at 36 years 8 months in 1985], 10 for England, a Lions tour in 1979, and 14 appearances for Yorkshire, whilst playing for Dewsbury, Leeds and Bradford; but at thirty-nine, what could he offer the Rovers? Fox knew his man, having coached him with Bradford, Leeds and Yorkshire, and needed him to provide the leadership and experience for the side he was building at Featherstone: and how his decision was vindicated!

Grayshon made his senior debut v. Leeds (at home) on 28 August 1988 and quickly proved that age does not matter if you are good enough and fit enough. Fox employed him as the king-pin of his pack, orchestrating short moves and feeding players with intelligent ball distribution. This proved very effective as the Rovers consolidated their position in the First Division, having been promoted from the Second Division in 1988. Grayshon's understanding with Deryck Fox was almost telepathic and his partnership with the up and coming Karl Harrison before his transfer to Hull was an effective combination.

Making a mockery of his age, he appeared in 34 out of 35 games in his first season, an ever-present 36 in 1989/90 and 30 out of 33 appearances in 1990/91 – 100 appearances out of a possible 104 games. On 5 November 1989 he added to his medal collection with a Yorkshire Cup runners-up medal as Bradford beat Rovers 20-14; and on 8 April 1990 he had the personal satisfaction of propping against his twenty-two-year-old son who played for Bradford at Featherstone (Rovers and Dad won 24-16). Despite this incredible record, the club did not offer him a contract for 1991/92, a decision of which Fox was openly critical. It

meant that Grayshon had played his last match for the Rovers v. Widnes (away) on 5 May 1991. He left Featherstone after a job well done and he then proceeded to notch up 104 appearances for Batley before retiring at the age of forty-five in 1995. He was awarded the MBE in 1992 for his services to rugby league.

His career statistics are remarkable enough, but his influence upon the Featherstone team and his durability in his early forties testified to his physical prowess, skill and unquenchable enthusiasm for the game. Grayshon gave much to Featherstone at an age when others had either retired or were content to serve out their contracts quietly.

Total appearances: 97 (+3)   Tries: 2   Points: 8

features of his game. His unorthodox running, which combined a stop-start action with a long, loping stride, was very effective and in 1967 he scored his 100th try, only the fourth Rovers player then to have achieved that feat.

He was leading try-scorer in 1960/61 with 20, and registered two hat-tricks against Hull KR (at home) in 1959 and Huddersfield (again at home) in December 1960. He scored some memorable tries, but reserved some specials for the Cup. At Halifax in February 1960 he scored in the 16-10 win; at Warrington in February 1961, his two tries contributed to Rovers' 13-10 win; and in 1967 his tries in the first round at Bradford and in the second round against Wakefield, were significant in the march to Wembley. It was the culmination of a career in which his appearance record was impressive. From 1958 to 1967 he averaged 30 per season and it meant that he was involved in all the RL Cup runs of 1958, 1959, 1960, 1961 and 1962, and the Yorkshire Cup finals of 1959 (the one victory), 1963 and 1966.

He deserved his 1967 Wembley appearance and how he revelled in the atmosphere – and this is the player who had an attack of nerves in the dressing room on his senior debut! His most significant contribution was in the second half, when he gathered a kick through by Tees, the Barrow full-back, on his own 10-yard line. He moved out to the wing, trampled over Tees who attempted to tackle him and then raced 50 yards before sheer numbers finally brought him down – vintage Greatorex. Off the field, he was the jester whose ready humour made him an essential part of the team.

Ken Greatorex had never played rugby league before the age of twenty-one, being a soccer player with Crofton Welfare until 1957, when he was invited to participate in a RL sevens tournament with Crofton. His team won and Ken had the thrill of racing 80 yards in the final to clinch victory. That experience whetted his appetite and he had trials with Featherstone. He soon impressed and was signed in September 1957, but his career had to be put on hold when he suffered a back injury and was not able to resume until September 1958.

After only eight games in the reserves, he made his debut against Wigan (at home) in October 1958 and was an instant success. He played in 31 of the 33 remaining games and went from strength to strength; he effectively never lost his senior place apart from injury. He alternated between wing and centre, but in either position it was his strong running and purposeful tackling which were the main

After the glory of Wembley, he opened the 1968/69 season with his 101st try in the 15-13 win over Hull, but four matches later he received the injury which eventually ended his career as he was forced to retire. In 1968/69, he was awarded a testimonial and the fans responded with £750. His effervescent personality was reflected in his play, and it always seemed that he was enjoying the game as much as on his first outing.

Total appearances: 282 (+6)   Tries: 101   Points: 303

Arthur Haigh is yet another of the Rovers thirteen who played in the first game as a senior club at Bradford on 27 August 1921. Although he took the loose forward position in his first two seasons, he settled more into the second row for the bulk of his career. After serving in the First World War, he was also a member of the successful junior side of 1919-21 which won eight cups in two seasons, and he readily settled into senior football. He was a no-nonsense, no frills player who shirked nothing and worked tirelessly throughout a game, using his strength in both defence and attack.

In the early seasons, competition for the back three rested between Haigh, Clements, Woolley and Barraclough, but he did play in the epic RL Cup-tie with Wigan in 1923. It was his solitary try at Widnes in the first round which gave Rovers a 5-2 win and set up the game with Wigan. He was more established in the side from 1923/24 as he made 38 appearances in 1924/25 and with six tries was the leading try-scorer amongst the forwards. He also made 38 appearances in the 1927/28 season in the gruelling campaign for league championship honours. As the work-horse of the pack, he made a significant contribution to the season. After a splendid League Championship semi-final victory at Leeds, the Rovers met Swinton in their only Top Four Final on 25 May 1928. Although under par, the Rovers were only losing 3-0 at the interval and Swinton themselves were uninspiring. Early in the second half Jimmy Williams broke through and passed to Haigh, who dropped the ball with the line at his mercy. It was just one of those days, but Arthur Haigh did not deserve it. He played in the Yorkshire Cup final against Leeds in the same year, but again tasted defeat. The nearest he came to representative honours was in October 1924, when he was reserve forward for Yorkshire v. Cumberland.

In 1929, he and Jimmy Williams were given a joint testimonial. In those days, a match was allocated. They chose the Bradford game and on a wretched day, the receipts were only £14! Fortunately, other efforts raised the final sum to £87 for each player. Haigh retired the following season after one match v. Wakefield (at home) on 5 October 1929. Although not spectacular, every team requires the work rate and solidity of players like Arthur Haigh. He served on the Rovers committee from 1945 to 1957.

Total appearances: 215   Tries: 26   Points: 78

Karl Harrison
Prop Forward, 1985-89

When George Pieniazek was appointed coach to the Rovers in November 1985, he immediately realised that a main requirement was to strengthen the pack and his first venture into the transfer market was to Bramley, where he acquired a young prop, Karl Harrison, for £15,000. Pieniazek only remained for one year, but Rovers fans saw the development of a future Great Britain international over the next four years.

Harrison's senior debut was at home to Warrington on 22 December 1985, and with the return of Peter Smith after a long lay-off shortly afterwards, the Rovers pack received a timely boost. The team was struggling to remain in the First Division, but a run of six victories in eight matches from March 1986 revived their flagging hopes and a 13-13 draw at Halifax on 20 April 1986 ensured their safety. Harrison played his part in this escape act but whilst his development continued in 1986/87, the Rovers were unable to repeat the act and were relegated to the Second Division.

Another excellent season for Harrison in 1987/88 saw the club finish second in the Second Division to Oldham, to seal an immediate return to the premier division which was the main target. Their attempts to land the Second Division Premiership Trophy were, however, also dashed by Oldham. The Rovers beat Wakefield in the semi-final in which Harrison scored a vital try in the 20-16 victory. In a thrilling final, Oldham snatched victory in the last minute to win 28-26, after Rovers had striven manfully with Harrison to the fore, to pull back a 22-0 deficit and take the lead 24-22. Both teams received a standing ovation.

With five tries (including a hat-trick at home to Barrow in April 1987) in 30 appearances, Harrison was now attracting attention as a strong, hard foraging prop who was also very useful in the loose. When Peter Fox signed Jeff Grayshon at the beginning of 1988/89, the Rovers had two commanding props as the mainstay of their pack and rose to a respectable sixth position upon their return to the First Division. Predictably, there was no success in the play-offs at the end of the season, although Harrison was still going from strength to strength, finishing his season in the play-off at Hull on 7 May 1989. The Rovers were now reluctantly resigned to losing their powerful prop and he moved to Hull in August 1989. After two seasons there, during which he commenced his impressive international career, he transferred to Halifax, eventually turned to coaching. After spells with Keighley and Bradford, he is now coaching Super League club Salford. He certainly fulfilled the promise which Featherstone saw in him originally, even if he peaked after he had left the club.

Total appearances: 106 (+8)   Tries: 16   Points: 64

David Hartley

Centre/Winger, 1965-76

David Hartley has the unique distinction of being the first substitute to score a try in a Rugby League Cup Final. Against Bradford in 1973, he replaced Mick Smith in the closing stages and immediately added his contribution to the Rovers 33-14 scoreline. It was his second Wembley appearance, but as substitute back in 1967 he was not called upon. In 1974, however, he was first choice selection as centre against Warrington in his third Wembley final. Unfortunately, he was the victim of a stiff-arm tackle by Murphy in the third minute and, as Warrington recorded a 24-9 victory, his winning sequence at Wembley was broken.

Hartley joined the Rovers from Leeds as a nineteen year old and made his senior debut at centre v. Hull (at home) on 29 January 1966. He made 16 consecutive appearances, scoring his first try in only his second game, and he was named a 'most promising prospect' at the end of the season. That promise did materialise and he spent the next ten years as an important part of the Featherstone set-up. He was equally at home on either the wing or centre and his strong bustling style made him very difficult to stop when into his stride. His career total of 116 tries puts him sixth in the Rovers all-time try-scorers list. He scored in the first three rounds of the 1974 RL Cup, his solitary try at Bradford in the third being the match winner. He also scored four tries in a match on two occasions, v. York (at home) in March 1969 and v. Whitehaven (at home) in April 1971. He was the club's leading try-scorer in three seasons from 1968 to 1971 and again in 1973/74. His best return was 19 in 1969/70 and 1973/74. In 1969/70, he appeared in all 41 games and had 66 consecutive appearances from December 1968 to 12 September 1970.

He was still prominent in 1974/75 with 10 tries, but thereafter his appearances diminished. His last game was at home to Wakefield on 2 May 1976 and as one would

expect from such a prolific try-scorer, he signed off with a try. He was then transferred to Rochdale. Once described as being 'like a centurion tank', he was extremely fast and used his bulk very effectively, although his all-round play would have benefited from more secure handling. He flourished in the Rovers back line of that time and was a very fine finisher.

Total appearances: 281 (+21)   Tries: 116   Points: 348

Frank Hemingway
Prop Forward, 1934-50

There is a strange consistency and longevity about the players who have worn the number 8 jersey at Featherstone, in that Ernest Barraclough was the first player to wear it in the opening league fixture in August 1921. From then until 1934, Barraclough made 304 appearances in that jersey. When he retired, Frank Hemingway took over and had 293 appearances until 1950 and was followed by Ken Welburn with 241 appearances until 1958. So, in a thirty-year span, three players dominated the position, which must be a record of its own.

Hemingway might have had the record of most appearances to himself but for the Second World War and injury. Signed from Streethouse Inters, he was immediately enlisted into the senior team making his debut v. Keighley (at home) on 10 November 1934 and instantly became a permanent fixture. When war was declared in 1939, he was working at Sharlston Colliery and was exempt from war service and so continued to play. However, later in the war he came out of the pit on the grounds of ill health and was then passed fit for war service and served in India. On a rare appearance at Christmas in 1946 he broke his leg at Castleford, which meant that he was only able to make 11 appearances between 1945 and 1949.

He was not a try scorer. It took him 68 games before he scored his first try at Hunslet in October 1936 and he only scored five tries in a career which lasted 15 years and 11 months – a club record until surpassed by Willis Fawley in 1967. He was, however, an outstanding prop and, according to the needs and demands of the game at that time, was the anchor-man of the scrum. Arthur Wood, Rovers' first international hooker, benefited from his experience and skill and very few players enjoyed propping against this gentle giant. He had enormous hands by which he bound his scrum opponents. He was particularly adept in loose play in bringing the ball away from his own line and, although not fast, he always managed to be in the right place at the right time. He was granted a testimonial in 1949/50, one of his best seasons, and he cherished the Yorkshire Cup final medal won in June 1940. He played six games in season 1950/51 and retired after playing against Barrow at Post Office Road on 9 September 1950.

Total appearances: 361   Tries: 5   Goals: 2   Points: 19

When a cheque for £166 was presented to Jack Higgins in June 1948, the heartfelt sentiment expressed was 'what might have been'. It was the proceeds of a testimonial which had been arranged following his premature retirement from the game in 1947.

Higgins made his Rovers debut on 21 April 1941 in the last game of that season at Hunslet. The Rovers won 14-2 and the display of the young scrum-half shone through. The club were playing in the War Emergency League during the war, and although the fixture lists were restricted, the Rovers managed to maintain a reasonable programme. Higgins scored his first try for the club against Batley (at home) in February 1942 and had established himself by 1943. He played in all 28 games in season 1943/44, and showed all his flair and skill in particular when he scored three tries against Oldham (at home) on 5 February 1944.

When peace-time football resumed in 1945, he had developed into a most competent footballer and his displays were attracting wider attention. As the Rovers struggled in a mid-table position, his play was a revelation and he was outstanding even in defeats against Bradford, Huddersfield and Halifax. His craft created three tries in the game with Rochdale in April as he inspired Rovers to a 15-5 victory.

Hopes were high at the start of the 1946/47 season. Higgins was appointed captain, but in a pre-season trial match he dislocated his hip and missed the whole of the season. Without his influence, the Rovers slumped to the bottom rungs of the table. He returned at the start of the 1947/48 season and was immediately in his best sparkling form, inspiring as captain, and representative honours were beckoning. Thus inspired, the team won its opening fixtures against Keighley, York and Castleford. In the fourth game, at Halifax, they were leading 15-8 with only 15 minutes to go when tragedy struck again. Higgins dislocated his hip for the second time and, as he was carried from the field, the Rovers crumpled and Halifax scored 19 points to secure a hollow 27-15 victory. Higgins's career was over and the Rovers plummeted to the bottom of the league. His was an outstanding talent and he varied his tactics around the scrum so that he bamboozled the opposition. An astute kicker with either foot, he was one of the most exciting footballers I have witnessed. It was a tragedy that the club and the game were deprived prematurely of such talent.

Total appearances: 100   Tries: 15   Goals: 13   Points: 71

J ack Hirst has been described as the 'prince of centres' and he graced the game in the first decade of Rovers' history as a senior club. His talent soon showed in junior football, attracting the attention of senior clubs, and he was actually spirited away and signed for the Rovers whilst Wakefield Trinity officials were at his house. That was in 1920 and he was therefore one of the Rovers thirteen who opened the club's senior history at Bradford on 27 August 1921. He soon settled to the senior game and enjoyed a full season, only missing 3 of the 29 games played. His first tries were scored at home to Leeds on 1 October 1921 when his inspirational value emerged and he so nearly gained victory with two special tries. The previous week at Leigh, Rovers had lost 25-0 but the *Athletic News* reported that 'Hirst is really a great centre with a fine swerve and plenty of speed. Although young, he is already a finished player'.

He continued his splendid form into the next season and was rewarded with selection for Yorkshire *v.* Cumberland at Maryport in October 1922 but had to withdraw through illness. This was the first indication of the injuries which were to blight his career. He eventually made his county debut in October 1924 and was only able to make four appearances in his career, which was a travesty. However, his 18 tries in 1922/23, was his seasonal best and included four tries *v.* Bradford.

In 1923/24, he was appointed captain but relinquished the position after one month as he was far happier without that responsibility. Although he had been unable to be the first Rovers player to play for his county, he did become the club's first international when he played for England *v.* Wales at Huddersfield on 1 October 1923. Hundreds of Rovers fans travelled to the game, but he did not have much opportunity to shine, allegedly 'with the half-backs wanting to go it alone'.

At club level the tries kept coming and in one purple patch he scored 10 tries in 8 matches between 15 March and 24 April 1924. He started the 1926/27 season in similar fashion and had already notched up six tries when he injured his knee at Batley on 6 November. This proved serious, and he was out for the rest of the season. He did attempt a comeback on the wing against Wakefield on 15 April 1927 which attracted a record league attendance of 7,000, but he had to leave the field with a recurrence of the knee injury. The club sought specialist advice from Sir Robert Jones of Liverpool who operated upon Hirst, although his fee of £70 caused comment at the next annual general meeting...

He did not return until 29 October 1927 and was thus able to assist in the club's bid for championship honours which ended in the League Championship final defeat by Swinton – but what an effort by the club in only its seventh season. What was encouraging was that Hirst was back and in devastating form and his efforts helped Rovers to their first Yorkshire Cup final in November 1928 – they lost 5-0 to Leeds. Hirst continued to excel and he scored five tries against Bradford

---

Total appearances: 277   Tries: 115   Goals: 3   Points: 351

Jack Hirst (second left) with, from left to right: F. Norbury, G. Whittaker, B. Gronow and J.T. Morris.

(at home) on 24 April 1929 – a club record which stood until 1968. His selection as reserve for Yorkshire signalled that the selectors were acknowledging his fight-back after injury, but then it all went wrong and another serious knee injury sustained at home to Broughton on 6 December 1931 ended his career at the comparatively young age of thirty.

The match accounts in those ten years are littered with superlatives describing Hirst's 'specials', which influenced so many matches. These examples give an indication of the maestro at his best – on 3 March 1923 RL Cup *v.* Wigan, 'Wigan were leading 11-3 when Hirst received the ball on the half-way line and threaded his way with characteristic swerve past opponents until Jim Sullivan was the last defender. His progress seemed halted, but he surged over to score. Another classic burst by Hirst gave Mason a try and then Hirst went over again only for the try to be disallowed and Wigan were mighty fortunate'. 24 October 1928 Yorkshire Cup second round at Fartown: 'Huddersfield were the league leaders and were unbeaten. Rovers were

21st in the league. With four minutes left, Huddersfield were leading 4-2 when Hirst picked the ball up from a ruck 20 yards out, feigning to pass he slipped past his opposing centre, a characteristic side-step disposed of another would be tackler, and then with a great rush left the full-back helpless and with a Huddersfield player hanging on, dropped between the posts for a magnificent try to win the match.' 24 June 1925 *v.* Warrington (at home), 'Hirst picked up the ball on the half-way line and with a characteristic run worked his way to within 10 yards of the line beating opponent after opponent before passing to Barraclough for Annable to score'.

He was a legend in his own time as crowds thrilled to his sheer artistry and football skills. His body swerve and side-step (he could manoeuvre a side-step on either side), were attributes which made him a truly great centre. The wonder is that, even in spite of his unfortunate injuries, he did not achieve more honours. Nevertheless, he lit up the Featherstone scene in its formative years and would have been an asset to any team.

He appeared in all 39 matches of that 1982/83 season, scoring 18 tries and in his sixth season with the club, fulfilling all the promise he had shown since being signed from the junior side. He actually made his senior debut at centre *v.* Castleford (at home) on 27 March 1978, but he soon reverted to second row and proceeded to carve out a most impressive career with the Rovers. He developed into a prolific try-scorer and his 21 tries in 1981/82 set up a new club record for a forward, and he was also top try-scorer in the First Division with 19 – the first time a forward had topped the list since two divisions were reintroduced in 1973. He was also an excellent goal-kicker, but with Steve Quinn around he never got the full opportunity at Featherstone. However, when Quinn was injured in 1978/79, he kicked 78 goals in 21 matches including two 10-goal hauls against Huddersfield and Rochdale – proof enough.

After impressing at Under 24 level for Great Britain against France in 1982, when he kicked seven goals in the two fixtures, he progressed to the senior team in 1984. His five goals *v.* France at Leeds were instrumental in their 10-0 defeat. He toured Australasia and Papua New Guinea in 1984, making 16 appearances and scoring 2 tries and 15 goals. He played in six of the Tests in a new position of prop forward. In the first, he came on as a substitute after 71 minutes and was sent off in the last seconds, for which he received a three-match suspension.

Hobbs's footballing brain, his speed, strength and bulk gave him every asset for success in the game and he used them well. His strong purposeful play was a rousing feature and his departure to Oldham in 1985 for a reported fee of £40,000 was widely regretted in Featherstone. His last match was at home to Widnes on 24 March 1985. Needless to say, he continued his successful international and county career with Oldham and then Bradford before finally turning to coaching.

W hen Featherstone Rovers pulled off yet another of their famous RL Cup upsets by beating red-hot favourites Hull by 14 points to 12 in the 1983 final, second-row forward David Hobbs's display earned him the Man of the Match award. He scored the first try from a well-planned move with Hudson and his second, late in the second half, levelled the scores. On each occasion, he caught the Hull cover by scoring wide with excellent positioning and powerful running. In between, he prevented Lee Crooks from touching down under the posts to save a certain try.

Total appearances: 172 (+33)   Tries: 66 Goals: 105   Drop Goals: 15   Points: 439

Norman Hockley

Second-Row Forward, 1956-62

Every team needs a Norman Hockley – the type of player who rarely hits the headlines, but who consistently turns out solid workmanlike performances and provides the solidity and power source to the pack. Featherstone were fortunate to acquire Hockley, whom they signed from Hull for £750 in August 1956. He made his senior debut on the following day *v.* Leeds (away) on 27 August and ironically then made an immediate return to the Boulevard in the Yorkshire Cup. The Rovers gained a surprise 7-6 victory, with Hockley leading the pack superbly and outshining his former colleagues. He 'ran like a second-row forward should and as the present breed at Featherstone do not'.

Hockley certainly provided that solidity to the Rovers pack in his first season and had a very effective second-row partnership with Albert Fearnley – each with their contrasting styles. Later, he alternated between prop and second row and was always dependable. Not being a spectacular player, it was perhaps inevitable that there were occasions when he was replaced by more expressive players but, inevitably sooner or later, the selectors turned back to him, and Hockley invariably responded. Occasionally (and naturally) he rebelled and asked to be transfer-listed, but it never affected his performances.

When not in the team he was certainly the best reserve to have around, and that was his lot in the Yorkshire Cup final of 1959 against Hull, when he gained his second Yorkshire Cup medal (he had played for Hull against Halifax in 1954). He did however, gain particular satisfaction earlier that year as he participated in the RL Cup run to the semi-final. He scored against St Helens in the emphatic 20-6 defeat of the cup favourites in the third round.

He made 32 appearances in 1961/62, his highest seasonal total, but with young starlets Ramshaw and Broom appearing on the scene, he again seemed to be on the fringe. In December 1962, in a complete reversal, Hull approached the Rovers for him to be transferred back to 'add experience and solidity to

their pack'. The Rovers agreed a concessionary transfer fee of £750 in recognition of his service – a gesture they would not have made to any other club. There he carried on in the same inimitable style and I personally thought that Rovers could ill afford to part with him at that time. Players like Norman Hockley are the salt of the earth and he served Featherstone well.

Total appearances: 172   Tries: 11   Points: 33

Terry Hudson
Scrum-Half, 1969-71 & 1979-84

There have been many talented scrum-halves who have left Featherstone because they were denied a regular senior team place and Terry Hudson was no exception. Signed in 1969, he made his senior debut away to Castleford on 7 April 1969, when he scored a try. The problem was, however, that Hudson was deputy to the outstanding Steve Nash and it was only in 1970/71, when Nash was injured, that he had a run of 24 successive matches. When Nash returned, Hudson was tried at loose forward but, understandably, he considered that this was not furthering his career and he asked for a move. He was transferred to Hull KR in October 1971 for a then record fee of £7,500. He had made 61 appearances in four seasons and had gained Yorkshire Cup runners-up medals in 1969 and 1970. However, the difference between Hudson and the others who departed was that he returned to Featherstone.

By 1979, Hudson had moved on to Wakefield from where he was transferred back to Featherstone in September, to regain his number 7 spot. Later, he switched to loose forward and when appointed captain in 1982, it was little realised that he was about to inspire the Rovers to one of their greatest triumphs. A low-key start to the 1983 RL Cup campaign v. Batley in the first round was suddenly ignited with a splendid second round win at Salford. Hudson scored in both games and then returned to the scrum-half berth for the third round tie at St Helens. He inspired his team to a marvellous 11-10 victory and was then equally inspirational as he won the Man of the Match award in the Rovers' semi-final defeat of Bradford. The rest, as they say, is history, as Hudson led the Rovers to their historic 14-12 win over Hull in an amazing final – despite being sin-binned for 10 minutes. Cometh the hour and cometh the man, and Terry Hudson reached his pinnacle in inspiring the team to those heights of 1983. He revelled latterly in his old-fashioned scrum-half role, but after Wembley he reverted to loose forward. In November 1984, he was transferred to Hunslet, where he only made 18 appearances in two seasons.

Always busy around the scrums, Terry had tremendous vision, could read the game well, spoiled the opposition with his terrier-like tactics, tackled well and was a well-respected and good captain. Ironically, he nearly missed his greatest achievement. The club were preparing to transfer him to Huddersfield before the start of the 1983 Cup campaign, but he decided against it!

Total appearances: 182 (+36)   Tries: 30   Goals: 3   Drop Goals: 2   Points: 99

Fred Hulme

Second-Row Forward, 1951-56

Fred Hulme joined Featherstone from the Old Pomfretians RU Club in January 1951 at the comparatively mature age of twenty-three. Initially he found it difficult to adapt to the rugby league game, but with an inherent talent and a willingness to learn, he was able to make the transition successfully. His senior debut was at York on 17 February 1951, when he deputised for Laurie Gant. It was Gant who patiently passed on his experience as Hulme improved his game and neither could have imagined that in a year's time they would be the second-row partnership in a team which was to shock the Rugby League world.

With his natural zest and enthusiasm, Hulme continued to improve and after a spell in the number 10 position, he reverted to the second row with Gant for the start of the 1952 RL Cup. Their efforts contributed to magnificent team efforts as both Wigan and Leigh were beaten as the Rovers progressed to their first RL Cup Final. Although they lost 18-10 to Workington, it was a wonderful experience which Hulme treasured.

He continued to impress and after a temporary loss of form in 1953/54 he developed into an outstanding forward with 31 appearances in 1954/55 and 35 appearances in 1955/56. His enormous appetite for work and lion-hearted approach were his main features and whilst he didn't score many tries, his forcefulness and thrust certainly created many for his colleagues. It was therefore a tragedy that as he reached his peak, he suffered a neck injury in the 7-7 drawn game at home to Huddersfield on 3rd April 1956. Although he managed to play three more matches to the end of the season, he was advised to give up the game. The club arranged a testimonial, but his premature exit was a great loss to the club. George Potts in the *Pontefract and Castleford Express* summed up Hulme's contribution as follows: 'Above all, he was a great trier and in many ways typified the Rugby Union

man's love of the game itself. He took a while to settle at Post Office Road but in 1955/56 his football showed a keenness, zest and skill which was worthy of representative honours. It was a great pity that his career had to finish when it did.'

Total appearances: 154   Tries: 7   Points: 21

If at first you don't succeed... Featherstone Rovers were originally interested in Jim Hunt in 1956. As captain of the Yorkshire Under 19 side, he had impressed in trials with the club, but instead he chose to sign for Castleford. Two years later, he was released by Castleford, and the Rovers backed their initial assessment and signed him. They were proved right. He was straight into the senior team at home to York on 5 April 1958 and he retained a permanent place for six years. His debut was impressive enough in that he virtually won the game with a splendid individual effort which gave him a try on his first outing. He scored 4 tries in 5 games and Rovers were more than satisfied.

He had problems with illness at the start of the 1958/59 season and did not resume until November, when he promptly scored again v. St Helens (at home). He was not, however, renowned for his try-scoring, although he did score a hat-trick against St Helens in April 1961. Most of his work was not entered on the scoresheet. He impressed as a solid dependable centre whose defensive qualities were outstanding. His partnership with Cyril Woolford was one of the features of the late 1950s and Woolford's try-scoring feats benefited from his service from Jim Hunt. They played together on 73 occasions sharing the euphoria of the Yorkshire Cup final win over Hull in 1959 and the stirring encounters of the RL Cup runs of 1959, 1960 and 1961, when Wembley was so cruelly denied – but some classic matches were left in our memories. The Rovers scored some thrilling victories where every player needed to contribute and Hunt never let the side down.

When Woolford retired in the close season of 1961, Hunt then partnered Ken Greatorex and newcomer Gary Jordan and was again disappointed to suffer defeats in another RL Cup semi-final, a Championship semi-final in 1962 and a Yorkshire Cup final against Halifax in 1963. A year later he played his last game at Wakefield on 3 October 1964 and gave up the game. His strong individualistic play and high tackling count must have taken its toll, but he contributed decisively to the Rovers' success of that period. Tragically, Hunt died in March 1969 after a long illness at the age of just thirty-one.

Total appearances: 167   Tries: 36   Points: 108

George Johnson
Full-Back/Stand Off, 1931-36

George Johnson had the distinction of being the only junior player to play for the Yorkshire amateur team (open age) in January 1931 against Lancashire at Oldham. His full-back display was particularly noted for 'his outstanding defence' and it was no surprise that the Rovers then signed him from their junior side at the end of that season. He was a versatile player and whilst he featured mainly at full-back in the early part of his career, he switched to stand-off in 1934 with equal success.

He had an interesting introduction to senior football, making his debut at home to Widnes on 19 September 1931. At that time, Jim Denton was the recognised goal-kicker, but two weeks later, on 3 October, the responsibility was passed to Johnson, who was making only his third senior appearance. He proceeded to kick 10 goals and score one try in a 47-0 home defeat of Bradford Northern and this match scoring record of 23 points was to remain until February 1964, when Don Fox scored 27 points against Stanningley. Despite this success, he was only occasionally used for goal-kicking throughout his Rovers career.

In the 1930s, the Rugby League organised tours to France to help in the development of the game there and Johnson became the first Rovers player to be selected for these 'RL XIIIs' when he toured in January 1935. He appeared in all three games in an unbeaten tour and, with five tries and four goals, was the leading points scorer. This season was also one of his most productive for the club and he made 31 appearances, his highest total. In September, he again played for the RL XIII against the French touring side Lyon-Villeurbanne at York. At this time the Rovers were languishing at the bottom of the league, not having won any of their opening five league games, and having succumbed to a record 60-2 defeat at Huddersfield. The secretary, G. Appleyard, took the unprecedented step of writing to the local *Express* asking supporters not to barrack the players, and particularly Johnson. A week later, Johnson asked to be placed on the transfer list and not surprisingly, he was snapped up by Hunslet, where he joined former Rovers, Winter and Plenderleith. The move was one which again eased Rovers' financial plight, but they were deprived of a talented footballer whose career perhaps unfairly suffered at Featherstone, because he was the son of the Rovers chairman, George Johnson (senior).

Total appearances: 103   Tries: 6   Goals: 50   Points: 118

Gary Jordan
Winger/Centre, 1961-69

A s Cyril Woolford, Rovers' ace winger, was moving towards retirement at the end of 1960/61, there was naturally concern as to how that gap could be filled. By coincidence, at the same time, a young winger who had been rejected by Wakefield was having trials in the 'A' team and made sufficient impression to be signed. He made his senior debut in the opening fixture of the next season on 19 August 1961 away to Batley, but he was injured and missed the next six matches. He resumed at Keighley on 23 September, when he scored his first try and by the end of the year he had scored 16 tries in 12 games. Furthermore, at the end of the season and having played in 37 of the last 38 games, he had scored 30 tries and incredibly in his first season, had failed by one to equal the try-scoring record of the

legend he had succeeded!

Their styles were different. Jordan was more subtle, almost gliding through the opposition as he utilised his undoubted pace. The try he scored against Warrington (at home) on 2 December 1961 was a typical example as he weaved his way at speed along the touchline from half-way to end up scoring under the posts. He continued to impress and by the end of season 1964/65, had scored 89 tries in 141 appearances. He almost played for Yorkshire in September 1962, but unfortunately pulled a leg muscle in the pre-match training session. He had more luck when playing for Great Britain against France in March 1964 when he scored a try in the 39-0 victory.

His creative and classy skills were, however, best suited to centre, and despite such success on the wing, and he moved to that position in season 1965/66. Half-way through the season, he gave up the game and began playing soccer with Ossett Town. He was persuaded to return a year later, in January 1967, and was immediately involved in the RL Cup run and saved the day in the third round encounter at home to Castleford on 18 March. Three minutes from the end of a pulsating encounter, Rovers were leading 8-4 when Hardisty, the Castleford number 6, scooped up an awkward bouncing ball on the half-way line to streak away towards an undefended line with a try looking inevitable. Jordan had the good sense to pursue and force him to score wide out. The attempted conversion was thus more difficult, failed, and Rovers has won 8-7. This aptly illustrated Jordan's anticipation and reading of a game and Wembley 1967 was the reward.

He played for Great Britain v. Australia at Swinton in December 1967, had a cartilage operation in 1968 and was eventually transferred to Castleford in January 1970. His last game was at home to Huddersfield on 19 October 1969 and his 115 tries place him seventh in the Rovers all-time try-scoring list.

Total appearances: 228 (+1)   Tries: 115   Points: 345

Cyril Kellett
Full-Back, 1968-74

When Cyril Kellett was transferred to his home-town club in January 1968, it was expected that he was in the twilight of his career. In eleven seasons with Hull KR, he had scored 2,527 points and kicked 1,211 goals to set up records galore, and it certainly was not anticipated that he would continue in the same vein at the age of twenty-eight. Six seasons later, he had rewritten the record books at Featherstone, played in two Yorkshire Cup finals and one RL Cup Final, and had carved his own niche in the annals of the club.

He made a low-key start with his senior debut on 20 January 1968 at home to Keighley when he kicked two goals and ended the season with 25 goals in 12 appearances. His impact was soon to be felt. In the opening game of 1968/69, he hit eight goals against Batley (at home) and the scene was set. He finished that season with 125 goals and would surely have repeated this feat in the next season had a fractured ankle against Swinton in January 1970 not ended a run of 38 consecutive appearances and a tally of 83 goals. He resumed in August to carry on in a similar fashion and records continued to fall. 10 goals and 2 tries (26 points) at home to Whitehaven in April 1971, fell one short of Don Fox's record club match total, but in an even more incredible season in 1972/73 he passed Don Fox's record career total of 503 goals and his season's total of 139 beat Fox's previous record of 129. The highlight of this season was his eight goals from eight attempts in Rovers 33-14 RL Cup Final win over Bradford at Wembley on 12 May 1973, which still remains an individual record for the most goals in a Challenge Cup final – and all at the age of thirty-four! A year later, he lost out to Harold Box in the 1974 final, having played in the semi-final, and he announced his retirement in June 1974.

Whilst goal-kicking records dominated his career, it should be remembered that in the twilight of his career Cyril Kellett resisted the claims of a young and very talented Harold Box for the number 1 spot, a tribute to his general play. A gentleman both on and off the field, Kellett supplemented his superlative accuracy in marksmanship with a quiet, unflappable approach to his game. He was not the quickest of players, but his ability and experience ensured that he was a master at running out of defence. His record of 557 goals has only been beaten by one player, Steve Quinn, and his final tally in a rugby league career stretching from 1956 to 1974 was 1,768 goals and 3,686 points. In the words of his adopted song, 'nice one, Cyril'. The Rugby League world was saddened by his untimely death in 1993 – a tribute to the affection felt for this great player.

Total appearances: 163 (+8)   Tries: 15   Goals: 557   Points: 1159

At 5ft 8in and 11.5st, Ken Kellett was not the largest of wingers, but what he lacked in stature he more than made up for in pace and determination. His style could have been likened to the modern-day Jason Robinson as a 'jinky' runner who could side-step off either foot and was strong and elusive.

He signed from Fryston Juniors in 1970, and made his senior debut at home against Bradford on 14 November 1970, when he deputised for the injured Hartley one week before the Yorkshire Cup final. Two years later, he had established himself and was playing in his first Wembley Cup Final. He did not score in the 33-14 rout of Bradford in May 1973, but he did notch up 18 tries and 36 appearances in that first full season. He married later that year and then stayed away when he could not regain his senior team place. He thus missed the 1974 Cup Final but, fortunately, he returned for the 1974/75 season and then played a huge part in the fortunes of the club until 1983. Between 1974 and 1977, he made 112 appearances out of 115, and with an ever-present 41 matches in the First Division Championship season of 1976/77, scored his highest seasonal total of 19 tries. By contrast in the following season, he suffered his only blank try season! He registered five hat-tricks of tries in his career and savoured the one he scored against his home-town club, Castleford, in the Boxing Day encounter at Post Office Road in December 1975. That was one of his most memorable matches. He gave away the first try, but recovered to score a splendid hat-trick and with an 18-18 drawn game, he sent both sets of supporters home happy! His final career total of 123 puts him in fourth place in the all-time lists behind Don Fox (162), John Newlove (147) and Jim Denton (129).

After the heights of the 1973 cup win and the First Division Championship of 1977, he shared the disappointments of Yorkshire Cup final defeats against Leeds and Castleford in 1976 and 1977 respectively. Two years after the First Division Championship, the Rovers were relegated to the Second Division, but bounced straight back in 1979/80. The following season, Kellett was granted a well-deserved testimonial and the pinnacle came when, against all the odds, he enjoyed another Wembley Cup Final run in 1983 which culminated in the 14-12 defeat of Hull. This was his cue to retire whilst at the top after thirteen dedicated years and at the age of thirty. In his last five seasons, maintaining his impressive consistency, he had scored 52 tries in 174 appearances. Sadly, he died aged just forty-one.

Total appearances: 353 (+7)   Tries: 123   Points: 369

There follows an extract from the Batley *v.* Featherstone match report on 20 September 1949: 'How he got himself into the forward mêlée which produced the try and finally barged over was as big a mystery as it was credit to his enthusiasm.' It describes the senior debut of Cliff Lambert, signed that month from the juniors, as a loose-forward but playing in the centre. Indeed, in his early days, his position could not be determined as he featured at centre, wing, second-row and loose-forward. An injury to Alan Sinclair prior to the start of the 1952 RL Cup campaign gave him the opportunity to stake a permanent claim on the number 13 jersey at Hunslet on 5 January and he never looked back. What was significant, was the match report comment that 'the introduction of Lambert at loose-forward seemed to produce more football than of late'. How prophetic! His try at Batley in the second round gave Rovers a plum draw against mighty Wigan, a game in which he played a significant part. After twenty minutes he failed to cover a bouncing ball and Hilton nipped in to score the opening try. Almost immediately, he atoned for his mistake with a spectacular forty-yard burst which paved the way for the try by Norman Mitchell. From then on, he completely outplayed his international loose-forward opponent, Harry Street, and Cliff Lambert had arrived.

Wembley 1952 was the first of many famous cup runs by the Rovers. The semi-final stage was reached in 1955, 1958, 1959, 1960 and 1962 and Lambert had the distinction of featuring in all but the 1959 campaign, when he had a cartilage operation. Against the cream of RL opposition, his presence was always significant and he invariably responded to the challenge. In March 1955, his try at Bradford in the second round disposed of one of the cup favourites. In the snow affected third round tie with St Helens in March 1958, he scored the solitary try (ironically created by former opponent Harry Street) which knocked out another cup favourite. At Swinton in the third round in March 1960, his famous 'back pocket pass' put Fawley through for the winning try and, two years later, he was the architect of the third round win over Leigh.

Whilst there was disappointment that his hopes of returning to Wembley were thwarted on so many occasions at the final hurdle, there was some consolation in a Yorkshire Cup final medal against Hull in October 1959 when he again scored a vital try in the 15-14 victory. By then he had moved into the second row to accommodate the young starlet Terry Clawson, and his partnership with Mick Clamp was one of the most stimulating second rows in the club's history. He enjoyed a well-deserved testimonial in that season and continued to excel with his special brand of football.

He scored 82 tries in his career, which was a club record for a forward until it was surpassed by Peter Smith in January 1987. The tries he made for colleagues probably exceeds that total. In 1953/54, he was the leading forward try-scorer in the Rugby

---

Total appearances: 376   Tries: 82   Goals: 3   Points: 252

Captain Eric Batten, Keith Goulding and Cliff Lambert (centre) in support of an unrecognisable colleague (with ball), in the RL Cup semi-final, Rovers 6 v. Leigh 2 at Headingley on 29 March 1952.

League with 13 tries, and he scored 9 tries in 10 matches between November and January. To follow this with 12 tries in 40 appearances in 1954/55, 10 tries in 36 appearances in 1955/56 and 13 tries in 33 appearances in 1956/57, underlined a consistent quality. What amazed many people was that the nearest he ever got to representative honours was a solitary 'travelling reserve' for Yorkshire. His efforts and talent deserved more.

Cliff ended 1961/62 playing as well as ever with a typical performance propping against Wakefield in the Championship semi-final, when Rovers were deprived of victory by a controversial decision to lose 13-8. Surprisingly, this was to be his last match. As he prepared for his fourteenth season with the Rovers in the close season, the club accepted an offer from Hunslet for his transfer. In his second game

with his new club he dislocated his collar bone and, in fact, he only played three games, the last being the 1962 Yorkshire Cup final between Hunslet and Hull KR.

Cliff Lambert was one of the finest forwards ever to grace the blue and white jersey. In a remarkable record of consistency, his whole success could be attributed to his exceptional natural football ability, which for him as a forward could even be described as classical. His characteristic dummy, his sudden accelerations, his subtly disguised reverse passes and his long quick decisive passes, served to open up the best defences in the rugby league and were all part of the neat quality football touches so uncommon in a player of such build, upon which his great reputation was built. He created so many memories for the fans to savour.

Ivor Lingard
Stand Off, 1961-64

The Sharlston area produced the Joe Mullaney/Don Fox half-back combination for the Rovers in the 1950s and early 1960s and it was a strange quirk that it should also produce their successors. Ivor Lingard had partnered Carl Dooler in the Featherstone junior side and signed for the club shortly after Dooler in January 1961. At a time when Dooler was having to be understudy to Don Fox, Ivor was in competition with Roy Bell as the contender for Joe Mullaney's successor, and continued to play with the juniors. Bell's transfer to Wakefield shortly afterwards opened the way and Lingard made an impressive senior debut at home to St Helens on 22 April 1961, playing in the last three matches of the season.

He first partnered Dooler at Workington on 9 September 1961 in an isolated appearance, but for both youngsters it was a case of playing the waiting game. Lingard's next opportunity came at the start of the 1962 RL Cup campaign and his sparkling display at home to Leigh in the third round established him as Fox's partner. Hopes of a Wembley appearance were dashed at the semi-final stage by Wakefield, but Lingard looked forward to his first full season. Unfortunately, he suffered a series of injuries in 1962/63 which punctuated his season, but he then returned towards the end and with Fox now at loose forward, he resumed his partnership with Dooler.

Described as another Willie Davies, the famous Bradford number 6, Lingard was deceptively quick, and although of slight build (5ft 7in, 10st 7lb), his defence was absolutely superb. He was the perfect runner for Dooler, which made them an extremely effective combination, and I am sure they would have developed into a great partnership. However, as Lingard demonstrated his excellent skills and ability in his first clear run in 1963/64, he announced that he was emigrating to Australia – and promptly played one of his best ever games in the 17-13 defeat of Wigan in December.

His last match was away to Huddersfield on 11 January 1964 and he was transferred to Parramatta for £4,000 – the highest transfer fee ever received by the club at that time. In his first season there, he played in all 28 games and reached the State Cup and Final play-offs. When Dooler met up with him on the 1966 Great Britain tour, he had played in all but two of the games since his arrival and had played in every back position – endorsement of his outstanding talent which the Rovers readily shared.

Total appearances: 69   Tries: 20   Points: 60

A s the Rovers attempted to emerge from the depressed 1930s, there was no more refreshing sight than the tall, dark, long-haired Albany Longley flashing down the touchline. He set Post Office Road alight with his incredible speed and some scintillating tries. Signed from Stourton Juniors, he scored 10 tries in his first season, after making his senior debut v. Bradford (home) on 12 September 1938, and 15 in 1939/40. Four of the latter were acquired in the Rovers' historic victory in the Yorkshire Cup competition in June 1940 – their first ever trophy. Longley had three tries in the second round 21-6 win over Bradford and he also scored in the final as the Rovers triumphed 12-9 against Wakefield. It was just the filip the club needed.

He served in the army during the war, which limited his appearances from 1942 to 1945, but when he resumed in 1945 he was soon amongst the tries. Two reports at the time on his progress were relevant – he 'had plenty of speed and initiative. Tackles in accordance with high tradition. Coaching in art of beating opposing full-back will improve his claim to high honours', and 'Longley in the army has learned to sidestep, which he will find better than crashing through'. This epitomised Longley. He had so much talent which was unbridled, partly because of his own attitude (he was very much a loner) and a lack of coaching. What he achieved was through raw application, but what a player he could have been.

He helped Rovers pull off a surprising league double against Leeds in the opening season after the war. His try at Headingley on 1 September 1945 contributed to a 9-2 win, and in the return match at Featherstone on 27 April 1946 he weighed in with two more tries in an enthralling 16-15 victory – part of a sequence of 10 tries in 9 games. His final total of 15 tries in 23 games endorsed his growing reputation. He also scored in Yorkshire's 13-10 win over Lancashire at Hunslet in November 1946, (he had made his debut appearance for the county in 1942). However, he was not settled at Featherstone and transferred to Wakefield in January 1947 for £750 – a record fee for Trinity. He moved to Barrow in 1949 and played against Rovers in a second round Cup-tie in 1950. He then returned to Featherstone in 1951, but only played six matches before retiring. His last game was away to Bramley on 11 April 1951 in what was almost an anticlimax, but he was certainly a shining light for the Rovers in the 1940s.

Total appearances: 457   Tries: 76   Points: 228

Paul Lyman
Second Row/Loose Forward, 1982-89

Born into a famous Featherstone family, both Paul Lyman's father and grandfather played for Rovers and so it seemed natural when he signed from the juniors in May 1982. He had the physical attributes – 6ft and 14st 7lb – and he also had pace which meant that in his early days there were occasional appearances in the backs. He soon established himself in the pack, where he thrived.

Paul had a daunting senior debut at Wigan on 26 November 1982, when Rovers lost 45-0, and whilst he only made nine appearances that season, he savoured the last which was at Wembley. He came on as a late substitute to share in Rovers' 14-12 win over Hull as one of the youngest players to play at Wembley (at 17 years 11 months). His play developed quickly from 1985 and he was soon attracting attention with his power and consistency. Apart from his speed and football ability, he could side-step and was difficult to tackle when into his stride. Not surprisingly, he featured amongst the try-scorers and headed the club list with 18 in 1985/86, (when he also won the Club Player of the Year Award), including a hat-trick against Widnes in the RL Cup. He also scored hat-tricks against Bramley and Sheffield in 1987/88 in a season's total of 17, which saw promotion back to the First Division and disappointment in losing the Second Division Premiership Trophy final to Oldham. In his many excellent games he was particularly outstanding in the 13-13 draw at Halifax in April 1986, which saved the Rovers from relegation; and his two tries sank Hull KR in the Yorkshire Cup second round replay in September 1986.

His ability was initially recognised at representative level for Yorkshire in September and October 1985, and then with Great Britain Under 21s v. New Zealand in October 1985 and France in January (Man of the Match) and February 1986. In his third game for Yorkshire v. Lancashire in September 1986, he scored a superb try after three minutes and 'went on to produce an excellent display of elusive running and strong tackling' as Yorkshire won 26-14. This prompted his selection as a travelling reserve for Great Britain in the first two Tests against the 1986 Australian tourists, but he never played.

After becoming unsettled at Featherstone, he was transferred to Hull KR in January 1989 for £55,000 in a deal which also saw Chris Burton join Featherstone. There he made 99 appearances and scored 39 tries. His was an immense, if perhaps slightly unfulfilled, talent.

Total appearances: 138 (+21)   Tries: 62   Points: 247

With only 157 appearances in 14 seasons, one might think that for most of his Rovers career John Marsden was on the fringe of the senior team. This was certainly true, but it said a lot for his determination and persistence that he stayed around long enough to make his comparatively brief but significant contribution. Certainly his commitment was never questioned, and he undoubtedly made the most of his talent.

Signed as a full-back from the Featherstone juniors in 1971, he had to live in the shadow of Cyril Kellett and Harold Box and spent most of his early years in the 'A' team under Brian Wrigglesworth. His senior debut was at centre at home to Leeds on 25 March 1974, but that was his solitary appearance and it was back to the reserves for most of the next two seasons. An injury to Box midway through 1976/77 enabled him to contribute to the First Division Championship. In the Yorkshire Cup final in October 1977, there was some compensation for the 17-7 defeat by Castleford in his Rovers Man of the Match award – 'He earned top marks for deadly tackling and taking Reilly's dive bombing kicks without flinching.' A week later, a broken jaw and depressed cheekbone against Hull KR put him out for the rest of the season.

He alternated amongst the backs until Box's departure in 1980, when he then appeared in every match (37) in 1980/81. He was, however, again ousted from the full-back position by Nigel Barker. Forever determined, he reverted to the wing and in a memorable purple patch, excelled himself in the 1983 RL Cup run. In the third round at St Helens he scored in the corner and he then created a try for Gilbert in the 11-10 victory, and in the semi-final victory over Bradford he again scored and then bumped off Jeff Grayshon to send Terry Hudson in. After Wembley, he enjoyed a testimonial season and received a then record £8,578 after which he retired.

What Marsden did not lack was wholehearted enthusiasm, courage, commitment and an unquenchable spirit. The opinions of fans varied on which position suited him best, but he used his pace and elusiveness to full effect and would have played anywhere – such was his dedication. His last game was at home to Halifax on 21 October 1984 – on the wing.

Total appearances: 130 (+27)   Tries: 23   Points: 69

Don Metcalfe

Centre/Full-Back, 1951-57

Few players can have experienced the meteoric start to a professional career which was enjoyed by Don Metcalfe. He was signed from Sandal RU in December 1951 as understudy to Freddie Miller, but was tried out at centre in his debut at home to Hull on 2 February 1952. Not only did he score his debut try, but he impressed sufficiently to retain his place and play his part in the glorious RL Cup run, although he missed the semi-final game. When he appeared at Wembley on 19 April 1952, it was only his 11th senior game, and eight days later, he played for England Under 21s in France.

Although national service intervened in 1953, this did not prevent his development as an outstanding prospect. One of his best tries was in the second round Yorkshire Cup-tie v. Hull KR (at home) in September 1952, when he went 75 yards in a classic strike and his defensive qualities were at their best against St Helens in February 1954 when 'magnificent tackling by Metcalfe was the feature of Rovers' 26-7 defeat'. In 1955 he had hopes of another Wembley trip as he scored three tries in the first round against Belle Vue and scored the all-important try in the 13-9 victory at Leigh in the third round. Those hopes were dashed in the semi-final by Workington who had also been the victors in the 1952 final.

He was appointed captain in 1955/56 at the age of twenty-one, one of the youngest ever for Rovers, and he thrived on the responsibility, leading by example. He also captained Yorkshire in his two appearances in October 1955 and September 1956. His 16 tries in 1955/56 headed the club try-scoring list. He had excelled at centre, but in November 1956 was asked to play at full-back. He had two games in the 'A' team, but then returned to the senior team – at centre! Seeds of discontent had seemingly been sown and in March 1957 he said that he would not play for the club again unless his transfer request was granted. The club refused, but in April he was transferred to Wakefield for £3,000, where he enjoyed another successful

career – at full-back.

He was hugely dedicated to the game and he excelled in both attack (with his eye for the opening and his galloping style) and defence. The *Pontefract & Castleford Express* said that Metcalfe 'has played some splendid football in a spirit which has always added prestige to the club. There is no sounder defensive footballer in the game and with an effective attacking edge. Had a tremendous capacity for work and retain the memory of many matches which he has won off his own bat, when all seemed lost'.

Total appearances: 149   Tries: 55   Goals: 1   Points: 167

It is perhaps difficult to envisage, with the passage of time, how one single player could have made such an impact in such a comparatively short time, but for those of us who were privileged to witness Freddie Miller's feats for Featherstone, he deserved all the accolades and respect he received. He was transferred from Hull in January 1950. His career with Hull had spanned 17 years, during which he had amassed 572 goals and 25 tries, but here was a player at the age of thirty-five who had been troubled with injury over the past 18 months and was unable to regain his place in the senior team. What could he do for Featherstone?

The answer was immediate. He transformed a young struggling team. In his debut match *v.* Whitehaven (at home) on 21 January 1950, he inspired the team to a 19-5 victory – their first win in 12 matches. He kicked 25 goals in 10 matches to end that season and then really burst forth in 1950/51. Appointed captain, his goal-kicking dominated as he initially broke Lockwood's club goal-scoring record of 57 in

January 1951 and went on to set up a new record of 97. His legendary kicking was now resurrected at Featherstone!

The arrival of Eric Batten as player-coach in June 1951 provided more experience and, together with a strong emphasis on physical conditioning and fitness, he blended the team into a formidable unit which excelled itself in the 1952 RL Cup. It was often said that if the team could prevent the opposition from scoring, then the Rovers would win because the opposition were unlikely to prevent Batten and Miller from doing so. Miller certainly kicked the goals and five against Rochdale and four against Batley saw Featherstone through to the third round for the first time since 1925. Mighty Wigan were routed in an epic 14-11 win with two towering drop goals and two conversions from Miller which sent the fans delirious. Against Leigh in the semi-final, Miller gave the finest kicking display I have ever witnessed. Faced with a gale-force wind in the first half, he completely out-manoeuvred his international full-back opponent, Jimmy Ledgard, and then stepped up to kick those three golden goals in the second half which took Featherstone to their first RL Cup Final. Although disappointed by the result, he came home to finish the season in glory when he reached 101 goals in the last game of the season at Whitehaven – not a bad return for a thirty-seven year old, and there was even a try to savour as he gave an outrageous dummy at York in January 1952, to slip past McLennie to total 11 points in a 14-3 win.

Featherstone was buzzing and eagerly awaiting the 1952/53 season, and the opportunity to build upon the Wembley visit. Miller was not, however, able to make his first appearance until 24 September, when his four-goal return gave Rovers a 14-4 victory over the Hull Rovers, and a semi-final place in the Yorkshire Cup. However, Batley secured a surprise 8-4 win at Post Office Road to dash the expectations, but Miller was back and kicking goals and there was much to look forward to… However, after 8 appearances

Total appearances: 92   Tries: 2   Goals: 245   Points: 496

Freddie Miller comes away with the ball against Workington in the RL Cup Final at an unfamiliar Wembley Stadium on 19 April 1952.

and 22 goals, Miller announced that his increased business commitments were taking their toll and after playing at home to Dewsbury on 22 November 1952 and kicking two goals in a 10-0 win, he effectively retired.

He was guest of honour for the match with Hull on 25 August 1956, when the reception he received in a ceremonial kick-off to the match confirmed the tremendous affection he had gained. It was known that he was in poor health and in July 1960 he passed away at the age of forty-five. In another endorsement of what he meant to Featherstone, his memory was preserved in the Freddie Miller Memorial Gate, which still stands as a fitting tribute to a great player and gentleman.

Contemporary eulogies from both the club and the local press at that time conveyed why he holds that special place. 'The way his records were achieved is the main reason why his name will live forever at Featherstone. He was the perfect answer to the Rover's prayers at the time for his goal-kicking, general guidance and experience from the full-back

position were the right ingredients to transform a struggling Rovers side into a more successful one.'

'It was not Miller's wonderful kicking which did the most for Rovers. It was his presence. A handsome man, big and strong, yet with a quiet personality, he was a gentleman on and off the field. He exuded confidence and it was confidence which the young Rovers team required then. The memory of Miller, imperiously marshalling his forces as the Featherstone line was under pressure from the best attackers in the game, clearing the line with ponderous touch finders and kicking difficult goals with the ease of the perfect stylist, will remain clear for a lifetime to those whose good fortune it was to see the born artist at work.'

Fifty years on, those memories have not dimmed. And for those without any memories of Freddie Miller, one simple statistic will suffice: in the 92 games he played for Featherstone he scored 48.3 per cent of Featherstone's total of 1,027 points!

speed and bulk, provided a new dimension to the Rovers pack. In 34 appearances, he scored 8 tries and had another successful season in 1964/65 which culminated in a typical try at Wigan in the Championship play-off which secured Rovers' surprise 15-8 victory. Sadly, he fractured his leg in the next round at Halifax and did not resume until January 1966. After playing in the 1966 Yorkshire Cup final v. Hull KR (another defeat), he was out for a spell but returned in time for the 1967 RL Cup run. His block-busting tries against Leeds in the semi-final when he took four defenders over with him and against Barrow in the final, when he scattered two defenders, demonstrated his power and strength and illustrated his worth. Complementing the brute force and power, however, was a shrewd football brain.

His impressive efforts gained recognition with a substitute appearance for Yorkshire v. Australia in October 1967 (the first of three appearances), and his play for Great Britain in the two encounters against France in February and March 1968 led to his selection for the World Championship series in Australasia in June. He played against France in Auckland and New Zealand in Sydney as well as the state games, scoring nine tries.

He was the club's player of the season in 1967/68, when he made his highest appearance total of 35 games. At Huddersfield in April 1968, he bounced off the goalpost to score another try and, in doing so, dislodged the crossbar, which had to be reinstated before the conversion could be taken. A cartilage operation in 1968 and a cracked ankle in 1970 restricted his appearances, but he was granted a well-deserved testimonial in 1971/72, during which he helped the 'A' team win the Yorkshire Senior Competition Shield. He played his last match, away to Wakefield, on 16 April 1972 and later joined coach Laurie Gant and Malcolm Dixon at York. Popular both on and off the field, his stirring play typified his approach to the game.

Physical attributes of 5ft 11in and 16st 10lb are more befitting a forward than a winger, yet Arnie Morgan was signed as a winger from Featherstone juniors in 1960. He gained experience initially with the 'A' team who won the Yorkshire Senior Competition Championship in 1961/62, during which it was suggested that he switch to the second row. It was in this position that he made his senior debut v. Bramley (away) on 17 February 1962, but then reverted to the wing.

He made his mark in 1963/64 after returning to the second row, when his block-busting runs, utilising both his exceptional

---

Total appearances: 233 (+11)   Tries: 49   Goals: 21   Points: 189

Joe Morgan must rank as one of the most versatile players ever to wear the Rovers jersey. Although he made 134 appearances at loose forward, he also appeared at scrum-half (30), centre (35), stand-off (34), wing (2) and second row (12). He made his senior debut at scrum-half at Dewsbury on 7 December 1921 in Rovers' inaugural season in senior rugby and was the fifth scrum-half tried. He remained there for the rest of the season, but then switched to centre and stand-off in the following season, and so the changes continued to be rung. It wasn't until 1927/28 that he settled to the loose forward position.

He had his share of injuries. In June 1923, his spine was injured in a roof fall at the local colliery and, having recovered from that, he was then out for most of the season with a rupture. He was also injured in February 1929 and, after returning in September, he had his jaw broken at Hull KR after only three matches. Despite this, he was the mainstay of the side for many years and with his versatility came an enthusiasm which was infectious. He revelled as captain in 1930/31 and in that season he inspired a great tussle with Swinton, the league leaders, in the first round of the RL Cup, narrowly won by the visitors by 7 points to 2. Playing at stand-off a year later in the same round, his brilliant play almost inspired a surprise win as Castleford scraped home 6-2. There was triple disappointment in 1928 as the Rovers were beaten in the League Championship and Yorkshire Cup finals and he missed out on selection for the tour to Australasia when many thought his play warranted a place. He seemed fated not to fulfill any representative honours. Selected to make his Yorkshire county debut on 28 January 1929, the fixture against Cumberland was cancelled because of the weather and because it had no bearing on the championship.

On 8 March 1930 at Huddersfield, the Morgan family created a record when the

team-sheet read number 2 Tom Morgan, number 7 Joe Morgan, number 10 Luke Morgan – Joe's brothers were playing with him for the first time. They appeared together on two further occasions in 1930/31. On 29 October 1932, Joe played his last game for the Rovers at home to Workington, at loose forward. It is difficult to imagine a more steadfast, committed and whole-hearted player who had played his part in establishing the Rovers as a senior club. He and his brother Luke gave great service, making 416 appearances between them.

Total appearances: 247   Tries: 19   Points: 57

of that season, and the first six of 1932/33 before being sent off at Halifax on 24 September and being suspended for four matches.

Ironically, during that period of suspension, he played for Yorkshire against Cumberland and was transferred to Halifax. He had therefore played in 126 of 128 games played by the club from 1929 to 1932. His transfer was yet another of the survival transfers which the Rovers had to make in the 1930s, but he did return from Halifax in 1934. He made his second debut *v*. Batley (away) on 2 December 1934 and immediately resumed his remarkable record, playing in all 20 of Rovers remaining fixtures in 1934/35; all 41 matches in 1935/36; and after a consecutive run of 66 matches, made 22 out of 25 appearances in 1936/37. His last game was at home to St Helens on 23 January 1937. It meant that, in his second spell, he had played in 83 out of 86 games, making a combined total of 209 appearances out of 214 games.

It is not incidental that Morris was also an excellent hooker who made three appearances for Yorkshire between 1931 and 1932. His sum total of two tries for the Rovers was achieved in one season, 1930/31, at home to Bradford and St Helens, but no doubt he was concentrating on all those appearances – some record!

There can be no apology for concentrating on the remarkable record of appearances held by Percy Morris, which is unparalleled in the history of the club. He was signed from Knottingley Juniors and made his senior debut in the opening game of the 1929/30 season *v*. Wakefield (away) on 31 August 1929. In a remarkable record of consistency, he then played in all 39 matches that season and all 43 in the next season; his consecutive run was only brought to a halt on 88 matches in the following season when he had to miss the game at Batley on 17 October 1931 because he was playing for Yorkshire. He then went on to play in 32 of the remaining 33 fixtures

Total appearances: 209   Tries: 2   Points: 6

Harold Moxon
Scrum-Half, 1938-46

There was no more fervent supporter of Featherstone Rovers than local cobbler Harold Moxon, who served the club as both player and coach. Signed from the local Girnhill Lane juniors, he made his senior debut against the all-powerful Hunslet team at home on 5 February 1938, to realise his boyhood dream. He made eight consecutive appearances in that season and then established himself in the following season and occasionally alternating with his half-back partner, Ray Hamer. He reverted to the scrum-half position for the Yorkshire Cup run of June 1940 and receiving a winner's medal after the 12-9 victory over Wakefield gave him his proudest moment.

Unfortunately, the war intervened and he was absent from 1942 to 1945 but he was back for the resumption of peace-time football in August 1945 and was appointed captain. Jim Brough reported at the time, 'Moxon played a real captain's part, here there and everywhere. His bursts from the scrum were reminiscent of Les Adams, the Leeds scrum-half. In defence, he was superb and gave an object lesson and inspiration to his band of warriors'. Unfortunately, in a freak accident at York on 25 December 1945, he collided with the touch-line fence and broke his ankle. When he returned on 28 September 1946 against Wakefield (at home) he was greatly affected by the tragic death of Frank Townsend, the Trinity centre who was tackled and carried from the field and died three hours later in Pontefract Infirmary. After playing at home to Batley on 12 October 1946, he gave up the game.

He took up refereeing successfully in 1947, but then turned to coaching. In 1957 he was appointed coach at Featherstone and enjoyed six highly successful years, showing the same enthusiasm and talent as before. The 1959 Yorkshire Cup final win over Hull was a triumph but Moxon was later philosophical over the great RL Cup campaigns of 1958 to 1962. On four occasions, injuries were instrumental in defeats at the semi-

final stage and in the one year when the team was injury free the Rovers lost through a controversial incident in the third round at Hull. Moxon deserved to take his beloved Featherstone to Wembley, but it was not to be.

Total appearances: 112   Tries: 16   Goals: 10   Points: 68

In 1953, when Joe Mullaney signed for Rovers from Sharlston Rovers, the club had finished the previous season in 24th position. From then and into the early 1960s, they rose from semi-obscurity to become one of the leading lights in rugby league and this rise was due in no small way to the part played by Mullaney. His half-back combination with another Sharlston product, Don Fox, became probably the most successful in the club's history and was a foundation of Rovers's success.

His senior debut at Bradford on 15 August 1953, shortly before his nineteenth birthday, was the start of a highly impressive first season. He played in 36 consecutive matches before missing the Easter Monday clash with Wakefield through injury. He returned the following day and was inspirational in a 15-9 victory over Huddersfield, scoring two brilliant tries. The brilliance and consistency of his play at such an early stage was remarkable and it came as no surprise that at the beginning of his second season, he was selected for Yorkshire against Cumberland in August 1954 and Lancashire in October. He scored in both games and helped Yorkshire to win the County Championship. Further honours should have followed when he was selected for the British RL XIII against Australasia, but he had to withdraw when he injured his thumb. This was the first of several ill-timed injuries which were to blight his representative career. However, he returned in February 1955 in the same impressive form which led to his appearance for England v. Other Nationalities at Wigan and another appearance for Yorkshire v. New Zealand in September.

In 1958/59, he was appointed vice-captain to Don Fox and when Fox was injured in December and was out for the rest of the season, the mantle of responsibility was passed to Mullaney. He responded superbly and in a three-year stint until 1962 he proved to be one of the club's most inspirational and astute leaders. He played one of his most memorable games in the third round RL Cup encounter with St Helens on 21 March 1959, when his two tries and one drop goal figured significantly in a magnificent 20-6 victory in a repeat of the previous year's 5-0 defeat of the Cup favourites. On both occasions, and as in 1955 and 1960, he had to share the disappointment of failing to achieve the Wembley dream at the semi-final stage.

There was compensation, however, on 31 October 1959 when he was presented with the Yorkshire Cup after a thrilling 15-14 win over Hull, the Rovers' first peace-time trophy. Two weeks later, he led the Rovers in an equally thrilling 23-15 victory over the Australian touring team – their first win over a touring side. 14 tries in that season was his highest season total.

His 41 appearances in 1959/60 and 38 appearances in 1960/61 were commendable, but by 1962 the strain of 301 appearances in nine seasons' football was beginning to take its toll. The arrival of starlet Ivor Lingard presented the first challenge to his position

Total appearances: 319	Tries: 85	Goals: 7	Points: 269

Captain Joe Mullaney in action against Hull at Odsal Stadium in the RL Cup semi-final on 11 April 1959. Cyril Woolford is in attendance and scored a solitary try as Rovers lost 15-5.

and Mullaney moved into the centre. Unfortunately, at Widnes on 8 May 1963 he received an arm injury which was to keep him out of action for the whole of the 1963/64 season. This was designated a testimonial season for both Fox and Mullaney in an appropriate joint venture. He did play in the last match of the season, but he then only made two appearances in 1964/65 as he passed on his experience in the reserves. His last match was against St Helens (at home) on 26 September 1964, the club against which he had starred in so many stirring encounters, and he retired at the end of the season.

In ten glorious years, he had contributed to a period where the Rovers had astounded the RL world with their cup exploits and had risen

to challenge consistently for league honours. His partnership with Fox provided so many highlights, but individually, Mullaney set an example of sportsmanship which was possibly equalled but never excelled. His skill and leadership helped many players develop as he led by example. In attack, his skill was rapier-like with an exciting change of pace, a very effective hand-off and a speed in seizing the slightest chance; in defence he showed split-second timing which no contemporaries could better. His representative career would undoubtedly have been longer but for injuries, and there really seemed to be no justice in him being deprived of that magical Wembley appearance on so many occasions. His stint for Featherstone deserved it!

Steve Nash
Scrum-Half, 1967-75

KR; Nash took the opportunity to stake his claim very forcibly as his successor.

He was an immediate success and his 1968/69 season was described as outstanding. It was followed by an even greater demonstration of his skills and talent as he appeared in all 41 of the games played by the club in 1969/70. He was consistently voted Man of the Match and finished second to Roger Millward in the Player of the Match competition which was introduced for that season. His exhilarating displays produced 14 tries and 17 goals and the only disappointment was the Yorkshire Cup final defeat by Hull. His first major setback however occurred in August 1970, when he tore knee ligaments in the home game with Wigan. He was out of action until January 1971, when he returned at Hunslet and his effervescent presence immediately inspired the side to register a 17-16 victory after four successive defeats. He scored a try described thus: 'and his peculiar mixture of style and strength left four defenders floundering'. His brilliant form paved the way for his international debut for Great Britain against France at St Helens on 17 March 1971, the start of an impressive Test career. He also made his debut for Yorkshire against Lancashire at Leigh on 29 September 1971, scoring a try in the 42-22 victory – this was the start of a long and successful career.

Success followed success as 1972/73 brought further landmarks. He captained Yorkshire in a 23-14 victory over Cumberland in September, scoring both tries, and he was then selected for the World Cup competition in France in October. He played in all four of Great Britain's games including the final when although drawing 10-10 with Australia, Great Britain took the championship with a better qualifying points record. At club level, he made 35 appearances contributing to a surge to second position in the league, Rovers' highest ever position prior to the switch to two divisions. The Challenge Cup victories over Salford, Rochdale and Warrington gave them a semi-final draw against local rivals Castleford. Nash had sparkled against Salford

As the Rovers progressed to their second Wembley final in 1967, a youngster who had been signed from the juniors that season was asked to deputise for regular stand-off Mick Smith in some of the league games before the final. That youngster was Steve Nash, who made his senior debut v. Halifax (at home) on 11 March 1967 and played five games at number 6. He was, however, a scrum-half and after the euphoria of Wembley, he settled down to being understudy to Carl Dooler whom, with Don Fox, had been his scrum-half idol as a youngster and that was the position he wanted. His chance came sooner than expected. Dooler was in dispute with the club midway through the following season, and then moved to Hull

Total appearances: 193 (+8)   Tries: 52   Goals: 70   Drop Goals: 2   Points: 299

Steve Nash seeks a way through in the RL Cup Final *v.* Warrington on 11 May 1974.

and Warrington, but he was the shining star of the 17-3 victory, and he followed this with another Man of the Match display in the 33-14 demolition of Bradford Northern in the final. His 'effervescent work in every phase of play' earned him the Lance Todd trophy – thus emulating his idol Carl Dooler, who won the trophy with Rovers in 1967. He was back on the Wembley trail again in 1974 as the Rovers progressed to their second successive final, but this time it was to be defeat at the hands of Warrington by 24 points to 9.

After Test duty against the Australian tourists in November 1973, he then departed for the 1974 tour of Australasia, playing in all six Tests against Australia and New Zealand and impressing with a Tour record of 16 appearances, 5 tries and 1 goal. He returned with a knee injury which severely restricted his club appearances in 1974/75. Although captain, he only made 11 appearances but such was his talent that when he did play, he inevitably dominated and scored 5 tries. More

international duties called in the World Championship series in Australia and New Zealand in June and when he returned, he asked to be transfer-listed and he was eventually transferred to Salford for a then world record fee of £15,000. There he continued to excel with more international appearances and for Salford he made 271 appearances and enjoyed a testimonial, before having to retire after an eye operation in January 1983.

In a quality line of scrum-halves, Steve Nash rates as one of the very best in the business, not only at club but also at international level. His strength to weight ratio was extraordinary. He used every ounce of his small stature (5ft 7in and 11st), which earned him his tag of 'the little big fellow of the team', to produce dynamic performances. He had pace and strength and shirked nothing. His almost impudent and exuberant style, laced with his swift acceleration, endeared him to many as he provided such entertainment with his talent and ability.

ated between wing and centre. He began the 1967/68 season comparatively late when he appeared at centre on 23 September 1967 at Wakefield. He had a run of 58 consecutive appearances which ended when he was injured in the cup game with Doncaster on 26 January 1969, during which he had featured 26 times on the wing and 32 in the centre. He was obviously adaptable and talented in whatever position, but coach Peter Fox wanted to get the best out of him and decided to switch him to stand-off in the home game with Whitehaven on 4 November 1973. Rovers won 31-17, Newlove scored two tries and Fox knew that the switch was worth persevering with. He gradually developed into a most astute tactician and with his exceptional ability to read a game he was in the best possible position to influence games. His uncanny perception resulted in many interceptions and his ability to accelerate from a standing position carved out many openings and the Rovers back line prospered.

He made his debut for Yorkshire at centre against Cumberland at Bramley on 12 September 1973, the first of three appearances. As an endorsement of his conversion, the last two appearances were at stand-off in 1975. Although an excellent captain, he eventually considered that it was affecting his play and he handed over to Vince Farrar. The Rovers now had their sights set on the First Division championship and moved to second position in 1975/76, when Newlove's 19 tries as leading try-scorer for the second time, were significant. The club wanted to go one better in the following season and Newlove again played his part with 22 consecutive appearances and 14 tries. As the momentum for the title chase gathered pace, he was injured at Widnes on 23 January 1977 and that was the end of his season. This was his first major injury and he could only stand on the touchline and cheer his team on to the First Division Championship. He was back in action the following season, his testimonial season, and added 14 more tries to his career total. He played in the opening match of

John Newlove almost played at Wembley in his very first season in senior football. He signed for Rovers from Ackworth in November 1966 and was enlisted straight into the senior team at centre on 19 November at home to Keighley. He was in the RL Cup squad and played in the semi-final against Leeds, but was then replaced by Jordan in the final. Any disappointment he may have had disappeared in 1973 when he returned to the famous stadium as captain and scored two tries in Rovers' defeat of Bradford Northern by 33 points to 14. He particularly enjoyed his second try, in which he started the move and finished scoring under the posts. He also scored upon his return in the following year, again as captain, but this time it was the bitter pill of disappointment as Warrington won 24-9. After the exhilarating final of the previous year, this ill-tempered clash was an anticlimax.

Although he established himself in the senior team after Wembley 1967, he fluctu-

Total appearances: 368 (+13)   Tries: 147   Goals: 4   Drop Goals: 1   Points: 450

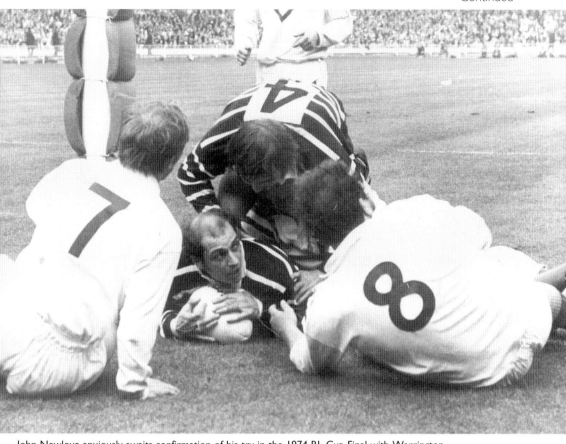

John Newlove anxiously awaits confirmation of his try in the 1974 RL Cup Final with Warrington.

1978/79 season at home to Huddersfield in the Yorkshire Cup, but was then transferred to Hull to join his former Rover colleagues Vince Farrar and Richard Stone (his brother-in-law). He played two seasons there and made his fourth and final visit to Wembley in 1980, when local rivals Hull KR beat Hull by 10 points to 5. This was his swan song as he pulled down the curtain on a fantastic rugby career.

John Newlove was an important cog in probably the most successful Rovers team ever in the glorious 1970s. Although he was disappointed not to gain a Yorkshire Cup final Winners medal after defeats in four finals – 1969, 1970, 1976 and 1977 – he gained many honours in his Rovers career. He was the first winner of the John Jepson Trophy in 1975/76, the club's Player of the Season award, and also shared the James Harrison Award for Yorkshire's fairest and most loyal player. He gave wonderful service to the Rovers and was well respected throughout the game. His career total of 147 tries is the second highest for a Rovers player (Don Fox had 162) and his 381 appearances place him fifth in the all-time list. Both these achievements are testimony to his football ability and loyalty. His best match return was four tries v. Batley (at home) in November 1971 and his best return for appearances in a season was 40 in 1972/73, the season when he also achieved his highest total of tries (21). Since retiring, he has used his experience in coaching junior teams and of course has produced three sons, all of whom have played for Featherstone – Paul, whose impressive career still continues with St Helens, Shaun, whose career was ended with a fractured leg, and Richard, who is currently with the Rovers.

When one considers what Paul Newlove has achieved in rugby league, one must be thankful that he chose this game and not football. As a youngster, he had trials with York City and no doubt could have gone far in the game. His phenomenal career began with the Rovers where his dad, John Newlove, had an outstanding career from 1966 to 1978. He signed as a seventeen year old from the Miners Welfare in August 1988 and soon made his debut on 27 September 1988 at Hull in the Yorkshire Cup, on the wing. Two matches later, his two tries at Warrington opened a try-scoring account which was to beat all records. It was already obvious that this was a remarkable talent and after 13 games the decision was taken to move him to centre where that talent could be even more effective – which is where he has rightly remained for most of his career.

The Rovers had just returned to the First Division and the main question was how this youngster would fare amongst the senior echelons. The question was soon answered. From the outset, Newlove displayed a footballing maturity which belied his tender years. As such, he made a tremendous impact. Not surprisingly, his first representative honour came on 20 January 1989, when he scored a try in Great Britain's Under 21 30-0 defeat of France at Leeds. Two days later, in the Rovers' 24-4 win at Halifax, he scored an incredible try. He broke clear from acting half-back 80 yards from the Halifax line and then twisted and turned both the Halifax wing and full-back before outpacing them, and the cover defence... In the next match at Whitehaven in the RL Cup, he was again Man of the Match, scoring two more tries with powerful running... Against Oldham (at home) in March, there was another outstanding 75 yard effort... and so it went on. 18 tries in 30 appearances in his first season and a glittering future.

Paul's success continued inexorably. Voted Greenall's Young Player of the Year in 1989, he made his Yorkshire debut v. Lancashire on 20 September 1989, on the wing, and within six minutes he had 'ghosted past McGinty and Hampson in high stepping fashion' for the first of two tries in a landslide 56-12 victory. On 21 October, he was substitute for Great Britain in the First Test v. New Zealand at Old Trafford and when he replaced Phil Ford after 76 minutes, he became the youngest ever Great Britain debutant at 18 years 72 days. He was a starter in the remaining two Tests, at centre, and his international career was well and truly launched. During the rest of his career with Rovers, his tally would increase to 11 appearances for Great Britain including the 1992 tour of Papua New Guinea and Australasia, 8 appearances for the Under 21 team and 1 appearance for England. Against France at Headingley on 2 April 1993 he scored three tries in Great Britain's 72-6 win, a performance described by coach Reilly as 'awesome'.

On the club front, he registered 18 more tries in his second season, but he was disappointed not to gain a winner's medal in the Yorkshire Cup final with Bradford in November 1989. The Rovers lost 20-14, but might have won? Newlove produced the best solo run of the game when he broke through tackles to race 50 yards, only for Bibb to miss the scoring pass! A series of niggling injuries disrupted his progress in 1990/91 and his presence was missed. He was

---

Total appearances: 150   Tries: 122   Goals: 9   Points: 506

Paul Newlove in typical action.

back to full production in 1991/92 with 25 tries in 32 games, but this did not prevent Rovers from being relegated to the Second Division for the second time. The one season in lower company saw Newlove hit the high spots with a flurry of tries. In November, facing First Division Salford in the Regal Trophy, he engineered a surprise 18-14 win and jinked his way past several defenders to score the decisive try. A month later his hat-trick of tries against fellow title contenders Oldham was crucial and Rovers went on to clinch the Championship. Against Bramley (at home) on 21 March 1993, another hat-trick of tries brought his tally to 32, equalling the club record of tries in a season by his wing partner Simpson, and a week later he set up the new record. As Second Division champions, the Rovers then finished the season in style by winning the Divisional Premiership Trophy final, beating a spirited Workington side by 20-16. Two tries by Newlove earned him the Man of the Match award and lifted his season's club tries to 48 and his full total to 52 – the first centre to score 50 tries in a season.

The inevitable then happened. Newlove's contract expired and after rejecting three new contract offers from the Rovers he was reluc-

tantly transfer-listed at a world record price tag of £750,000. In July he joined Bradford Northern for £245,000 – a price determined by the RL tribunal. Understandably, he wanted to achieve more in the game and that he has done with Bradford and then St Helens from November 1995. Although he has now retired from international football, he remains a force at club level.

As a footballer, Newlove has everything. He has pace, swerve and side-step, which allied to his bulk makes him a formidable player. When he started playing, he was 13.5 stone, but as his weight increased to 15 stone, it only added to his armoury. As he has proved time and time again, 15 yards from the line he is particularly a power as he uses all his attributes with immense upper-body strength. How many tries he has scored is one thing – how many he has made for others is equally relevant. With his defensive qualities, he is the complete footballer and one of the outstanding players of his era. Many have described him as another Neil Fox, the outstanding Trinity centre of the 1950s and 1960s. He is certainly the only player who has earned that comparison, which is praise indeed.

There have been a few players at Featherstone who could be classed as 'points machines', but in the period up to the onset of the Super League era, Martin Pearson tops the list. His 1,338 points in 166 matches gave him a match average of 8.06, as compared to Steve Quinn's average of 6.79, with 2,656 points from 391 matches. Jamie Rooney, who is currently playing, has a better average of 10.45 but his career has yet to be concluded.

Although Pearson made his senior debut away to Oldham on 5 March 1989, after a substitute appearance at home to Wigan the previous week, he did not burst upon the senior scene until 1990/91. As can beset a utility player, versatility can be a hindrance in determining a best position, but with Pearson the consensus seemed to rest between full-back and stand-off. Strangely, his points-scoring ability did not emerge until 1992/93, when the Rovers found themselves in the Second Division. They bounced back at the first attempt with only three defeats and amassing 996 points in their league campaign. Pearson took full advantage to set up a new club season record of 391 points (28 tries, 139 goals, 1 drop goal). Back in the First Division he continued in the same style with 267 points in 1993/94, 233 in 1995/96 and 231 in 1996. This included a club match record of 40 points (12 goals, 4 tries) *v*. Whitehaven on 26 November 1995. He missed out in 1994/95 when he was injured *v*. Bradford in only his fifth match and was out for the rest of the season. In 1996, he scored in every game he played (20 out of 21).

At Under 21 level, his prolific scoring was maintained for Great Britain. He made his debut *v*. Papua New Guinea on 30 October 1991 with eight goals and with matches against France in 1992 and 1993, amassed a total of 24 goals and 4 tries. He holds the match records for most points (3 goals, 6 tries – 24), goals (8) and tries (3). His injury in 1994 scuppered his hopes of playing against the touring Australians.

When Rovers failed to gain promotion to Super League in 1996, he was transfer-listed and eventually joined Halifax in December. He then played for Wakefield and is now reported to be playing Rugby Union in France. In such a comparatively short career he certainly left his mark with the Rovers. An all-round player, he was particularly quick over twenty to thirty yards, an exciting attacking player and an excellent tactical player as well as goal kicker.

Total appearances: 148 (+18)   Tries: 101   Goals: 464   Drop Goals: 8   Points: 1338

Steve Quinn

Centre, 1976-88

Throughout the history of Featherstone Rovers there has been a tendency in their transfer dealings for the big signings to be relatively unsuccessful and the more modest signings to be excellent value for money. Steve Quinn must rate as the bargain of the century. In January 1976 his career with home-town York had stalled after 353 goals and 117 appearances in a five-year stint. He did not wish to play again for York and had been transfer-listed at £500. Rovers coach Keith Goulding recommended that the Rovers sign him and in his first outing with the reserves at Hull KR he kicked five goals out of six, and prompted the Rovers official with the team to insist that he be brought straight into the senior team – he was. On his debut at home to Wakefield in the first round of the Challenge Cup on 15 February 1976, he kicked four goals in the 23-9 win and the Steve Quinn phenomenon had begun.

He scored 3 tries and 39 goals in 10 appearances in his first season as Rovers finished runners-up in the First Division. In the following season, they surpassed themselves. Although there was initial disappointment in yet another Yorkshire Cup final defeat, against Leeds in October, with a rampant pack and lively backs and the unswerving consistency of Quinn's goal-kicking, they took the First Division title for the first time in their history. Quinn played in all 41 games setting up new records for goals (152) and points (328) scored and equalling Tommy Smales fastest century of points in nine matches. After the excellence of 1977, it was almost unbelievable that the Rovers should be relegated to the Second Division two years later, but the absence of Quinn, who only made 14 appearances, was significant.

The team bounced back in fine style as Second Division champions in 1979/80, with Steve Quinn again to the fore with another record-breaking season. He broke his own club records for goals (163) and points (375) in a season (and headed the League's lists), and set up new records by playing and scoring in all 31 games, and scoring 29 points (10

goals and 3 tries) against Doncaster in November 1979 (beating Don Fox's record of 27). He also equalled the record for the fastest century of goals in 18 games, shared with David Watkins of Salford and Bernard Ganley of Oldham. Not surprisingly, he won both the Second Division and the club's Player of the Year awards.

And there was more. He continued into 1980/81 and 1981/82 with two more centuries of goals (115 and 119) which helped the Rovers retain their First Division status. His four goals v. Castleford in August 1981 enabled him to break Cyril Kellett's record 557 goals for the club. His three goals against Warrington meant that he had overhauled Don Fox's all-time record of 1,492 career points, but there was even more glory at the end of that 1982/83 season. Against the odds, the Rovers again confounded the critics by reaching the 1983 Cup Final to meet Hull,

---

Total appearances: 381 (+10)   Tries: 75   Goals: 1200   Drop Goals: 10   Points: 2656

Apart from all that goal-kicking, Steve Quinn also scored 75 tries.

already League Champions and red hot favourites against a team occupying a 14th position in the League. After a lean spell with his marksmanship (by his standards), Quinn missed his first touchline kick after Hobbs's try before hitting three out of three. With three minutes to go and the scores level, Rovers were awarded another penalty and calm and collected (outwardly at least), Quinn stepped up to kick his fourth goal and win the match as well as writing another chapter in his Rovers career.

The points kept coming with another century of goals (127) in 1987/88 (with 10 goals and two tries against his former club), after which he was the first recipient of the club's Keith Goulding Clubman of the Year award. What effect this points-scoring had on representative calls was confined to Yorkshire. He made his county debut on 5 October 1977 and kicked five goals in the 28-10 defeat of Cumberland, ironically at York. He made five more appearances up to 1981, with a total of 14 goals.

He was granted a testimonial in 1986/87 and the Rovers fans demonstrated how much they appreciated his efforts with a record £13,000. By 1988 at the age of thirty-five and with 19 seasons in football, 14 of which were with the Rovers, he decided to call it a day. His last full match was away to Widnes in the John Player competition on 13 November 1988 where he signed off with two more goals; he made his final farewell as substitute at Leeds on 11 December. Whilst the emphasis understandably has been on his points-scoring, Quinn was an accomplished footballer and although essentially a defensive centre, he still managed to score 75 tries. His goal-kicking marksmanship speaks for itself and yet he apparently never practised. Five months after his retirement he was surprised at a gathering at Post Office Road when presentations were made to him for his achievements – an indication of the affection for Featherstone's adopted son and a tribute to a remarkable sportsman.

Terry Ramshaw
Second-Row Forward, 1960-65

Fred Hulme, the former Rovers second-row forward, recommended Terry Ramshaw to Featherstone and I suppose it takes a good second-row forward to know one. Signed from the Castleford junior side in 1960, he made his senior debut at Batley on 19 August 1961 at the age of seventeen. He immediately impressed, but after two matches his progress was marred by a series of injuries; fortunately, he was able to return in time for the Challenge Cup. He confirmed his promise with some powerful performances, particularly against Leigh in the third round and in the disappointing semi-final defeat against Wakefield.

Ramshaw maintained his progress in 1962/63 and by 1963 he was showing extra-ordinary maturity for a youngster in the powerhouse of the pack. At 6ft and 14st 12lb, his strong powerful play and forceful runs were a feature and he particularly excelled against the Australian tourists in an outstanding 23-17 win on 2 October 1963, when he ripped the Aussie defence open with a typical try. His hopes of a Yorkshire Cup winner's medal were dashed a month later when an off-form Rovers surprisingly slumped to a 10-0 defeat by Halifax. Worse was to follow. A back injury at Huddersfield on 11 January 1964 brought his season abruptly to an end as he was placed in a plaster cast.

He returned to display his best form in 1964/65 with 10 tries in 31 appearances (he was runner-up in the season's try scoring list), and formed a formidable second-row partnership with Arnie Morgan. He was in dynamic form away to Hunslet on 13 February 1965 when he repeatedly tore out of tackles to score and also created one for Jordan. Such form was recognised in his selection for Great Britain Under 24 *v.* France at Toulouse on 3 April 1965, and it was a triumphant climax to his come-back after the previous season's long lay-off. In the close season, however, he expressed a wish to move to a better club and was briefly transfer-listed at a then club record fee of

£10,000. The club hoped that he had settled, but there was further dispute and after playing at Widnes on 9 October 1965 he was transferred to Halifax in November for a then club record of £5,000. He had outstanding talent, combining aggression with skill and never shirking in all-out effort. He enjoyed further success with Bradford and Salford. His son Jason has served Keighley well for many years.

Total appearances: 100   Tries: 27   Points: 81

In 1974 however, they were not allowed as much scope against the Warrington side and were beaten 24-9 in a disappointing game.

Signed from Featherstone juniors in January 1968, Rhodes made his senior debut at home to Hunslet on 2 March 1968, one of three appearances he made that season. There was strong competition amongst the forwards with Arnie Morgan, Jimmy Thompson, Stan Nicholson and Steve Lyons in full flow and he had the occasional game at prop, but with some players departing he was able to establish himself in the early 1970s. He had scored his first try at Bramley in September 1968, but as his style developed, more opportunities for tries emerged and he took them. He had pace and with his roving commission he was always in support of colleagues like Keith Bell to take the short ball and go through the gap. His characteristic diagonal running as he tore through defences, thrilled the crowds and with 15 tries in 1971/72 and 14 in 1972/73, he was amongst the club's leading try-scorers. He had a hat-trick at home to Doncaster on 27 December 1971, when he was in outstanding form.

Apart from his Wembley medals, he also played in the Yorkshire Cup final *v.* Leeds in November 1970 and the Captain Morgan Trophy final against Warrington in January 1974, both games ending in defeat for the Rovers. With a re-shaped pack emerging in the mid-1970s – a pack which was to be the driving force of the First Division – he realised his chances would be more limited and he moved to Castleford for £2,500 in January 1975. There, he had a brief career, making only 13 appearances. He later turned to coaching at York, Doncaster and Sheffield.

W hen coach Peter Fox took Rovers to Wembley in successive seasons in 1973 and 1974, one of his declared requirements was that you need running forwards at Wembley. He had chosen Alan Rhodes in his 1973 side and in 1974, with competition from Busfield, he again selected Rhodes for his ability to run, particularly out wide. Against Bradford in the 1973 final, Rhodes's style was most effective in the first half when, having chosen the running game, Rovers powered in for 17 points in the first 20 minutes to lay the foundations for an emphatic 33-14 victory.

Total appearances: 153 (+37)   Tries: 53   Goals: 1   Points: 161

Jamie Rooney
Scrum-Half, 1998-present

Following in the best tradition of points-scoring scrum-halves at Featherstone, it will be intriguing to see what the future holds for Jamie Rooney as he seeks to further his football career. At the end of June 2002, the deadline for this publication, he had kicked 451 goals, including 35 drop goals and amassed 1,087 points in only 104 appearances. As such, he is already poised to challenge the record of his illustrious predecessors at Featherstone.

He was only eighteen when he made his first Rovers appearances in the Treize Tournoi tournament held in October 1998 which involved French and English RL clubs. He made substitute appearances at Limoux and at home to St Esteve before his full debut at St Esteve on 18 October 1998. He kicked two goals and had had a satisfactory introduction to senior football. Versatile half-back Handley was however, in the number 7 spot at the beginning of the 1999 season, as Rooney continued to gain experience in the reserves but, midway through the season, it was decided to move Handley to stand-off and give the young Rooney an extended run at scrum-half. He reappeared away to Doncaster on 16 May 1999 and the Rovers realised that they had a young star in their midst who could also score points. In 19 appearances in his first full season, he scored 172 points (9 tries and 72 goals) and he followed this with 331 points in 1999/00. Apart from his scoring feats, he displayed a maturity in his play, where his intelligent running and astute kicking showed great potential for the future. His touches were those of a natural footballer and he was named Northern Ford Premiership Player of the Year as well as Club Player of the Year. He took on the responsibility of captain in 2000/01 and obliged with 307 more points in 27 matches. The only blemish occurred at York on 4 February 2001, when he was the victim of a vicious late tackle which fractured his jaw. He was out for five weeks and returned to kick eight goals and one try in the home

game with Chorley. In 2001, he had a month's trial with Super League club Castleford and newly-promoted Widnes showed some interest, but nothing materialised and Featherstone continue to have the benefit of his extraordinary scoring feats. At 30 June 2002, his 1,087 points in 104 matches gave him an average of 10.45, the best return by a Rovers player. Whether his talent eventually leads to Super League football remains to be seen but, in the meantime, his records at NFP level mount-up.

Total appearances: 100 (+4) Tries: 55 Goals: 416 Drop Goals: 35 Points: 1087 (until 06/02)

Billy Banks, the Wakefield international scrum-half. A run of 24 successive defeats must have been soul destroying, but Russell was always cajoling and prompting The situation did not improve much in 1948/49, but Russell enjoyed his best season with 31 appearances and 8 tries.

Full of enthusiasm and endeavour, he withstood the challenge of Cyril Gilbertson in 1949/50 and with the arrival of Freddie Miller there was some relief as his superb kicking lifted the pressure. Totally unpredictable, Russell's unorthodox style did have its rewards. His try at Castleford in November 1950 earned a shock 16-15 win against his home-town club, and against York in April 1951 his try prompted this report: 'Russell's individuality is still the subject of much comment. To score his try he went straight through the pack from 10 yards out with physical strength not associated with number 7s'. Laurie Gant, who played with him, recalls that often when he got the ball from the scrum he would say 'follow me'. Laurie did, and nothing happened as Jimmy went on his own individual way. He was tough and uncompromising, but was a shining light for the Rovers. Jack Blackburn and Russell shared a testimonial in 1951/52, but when he was replaced by Ray Evans in the 1952 Cup run, he parted company with Featherstone. His last game was at home to Dewsbury on 29 December 1951 and after a brief spell at Hull KR, he gave up the game.

The Rovers did not have much to cheer about in the late 1940s, but one player who brought colour and character to the side was Jimmy Russell. His ruddy complexion and jaunty air were striking, and he had a very unusual style with his bowed legs, which earned him the nickname of 'cowboy'. It was often joked that he ran on his knees!

He joined the club as a stand-off in 1938, but soon reverted to scrum-half and made his senior debut at Hull on 1 April 1939. He made only two appearances before the outbreak of war in September intervened, and he did not return until after the war, which took six years out of his career. Jack Higgins and Harold Moxon had established themselves in the meantime and were vying for the number 7 position which meant that Russell had to spend his time with the reserves. Their retirement gave him his opportunity in 1947/48 and as the Rovers struggled in the league, his two tries against Wakefield in a surprise 19-11 win in October brought some relief. This was one of his most satisfying games as he outplayed

---

Total appearances: 128   Tries: 26   Goals: 7   Points: 92

Bill Sherwood
Loose Forward, 1935-45

Bill Sherwood commenced his senior career with Bradford Northern when he signed as a youngster from Castleford British Legion. At that time he was an aspiring stand-off, but when he was transferred to Featherstone in September 1935 he had moved to loose forward. He would remember his debut for the Rovers. At Huddersfield on 21 September 1935, the home side inflicted upon the Rovers their heaviest defeat in their senior club history – 60-2. It was certainly no picnic as Rovers only won five games in both 1935/36 and 1936/37, and had 625 and 858 points respectively scored against them as they languished at the bottom of the table.

Undeterred, Bill Sherwood's tough, gritty play was suited to this situation and after 33 appearances in his first season, he led the Rovers with conviction and brought some relief with his goal-kicking. He topped both the club goal and points-scoring lists for six successive seasons from 1936 to 1942 and in dismal seasons, his best efforts were five goals and one try which brought a surprise 16-11 home win against Huddersfield in April 1937 and six goals and one try *v.* Rochdale (at home) in October 1937. Yet he stuck at it and when the club was revived by a new policy in 1937, he was there to guide the 'new order' to better days. His deserved reward was a Yorkshire Cup final medal when Rovers beat Wakefield in the 1940 final to gain their first trophy. Significantly, he was to play a full part with a try and three goals in the first round, and three goals in each of the succeeding matches against Bradford, Dewsbury and Wakefield. In the final, he led the forwards in fine style and was involved in the first try. Half-way through the second half, his glorious touch-line penalty kick gave Rovers the lead 10-9 and he then added a drop goal in the closing stages to conclude the scoring.

A hard, uncompromising player with his characteristic skull cap, Sherwood was just the player Rovers needed to surmount those dark days of the 1930s. He played through the war, but then decided to retire after one game in the 1945/46 season at Dewsbury on 22 November 1945. He was then appointed coach until 1947 and returned for a second stint from 1948 to 1951 as Rovers' fortunes began to pick up. He was succeeded by Eric Batten and had a brief spell on the Rovers committee, concluding what was a whole-hearted dedication to the Rovers.

Total appearances: 205   Tries: 33   Goals: 236   Points: 571

Gary Siddall ———————————————————————————
Prop Forward, 1978-89

His initial attempts to establish himself as a regular were thwarted by injury. At the beginning of 1980/81, he broke an ankle at home to Barrow and was out for four months; torn ligaments at Wigan in November 1982 ended a run of 41 consecutive appearances. He returned in March in time to play his part in the RL Cup victories over St Helens and Bradford but Mick Gibbins got the nod for the line-up against Hull in the final. He came on as substitute in the closing stages and was involved in the movement which led to David Hobbs's second try and celebrated Rovers' remarkable victory. He consolidated his position over the next two seasons making his most appearances (33) and most tries (6) in 1984/85. Then playing against Halifax (at home) on 20 October 1985, he broke two bones in his back and was out for 16 months. With typical determination, he resolved to return and after one nostalgic appearance in February 1987 he made a triumphant comeback at York on 2 September 1987. The Rovers were then back in the Second Division but he completed one of his finest seasons making 33 appearances and taking part in the dramatic Second Division Premiership Trophy final against Oldham at Old Trafford when Rovers lost 28-26. For Gary Siddall it was a remarkable triumph over his adversity and he was rewarded with a well-deserved testimonial. His last full game was at home to Bradford on 2 October 1988, but he was substitute at Castleford on 24 March 1989. During that season he led the successful Alliance team before transferring to Huddersfield in October 1989.

Known affectionately as the Gentle Giant, Siddall was a dedicated club-man whose loyalty and commitment were key virtues. A solid prop, he had a good pair of hands and was always looking to off-load. He gained widespread respect and admiration for the courage and determination he showed in overcoming serious injuries. He evidently loved the game in general and Rovers in particular.

Gary Siddall's dilemma in 1978 was whether to pursue a career in the Royal Navy or with Featherstone Rovers. It was whilst he was on leave from the navy in 1977 (where he played rugby union for United Services, Portsmouth), that he was persuaded to have trials with the club. He impressed sufficiently for the club to maintain contact and in August 1978 he signed, made his senior debut at home to Widnes on 10 September 1978 and then left for his final tour of duty with the navy. When he returned, the club had been relegated to the Second Division but he played in five of the last games of the season as their immediate return as Second Division champions was celebrated.

Total appearances: 167 (+20)   Tries: 25   Points: 90

Owen Simpson
Winger, 1990-96

With the money acquired from their record transfer fee for Graham Steadman upon his move to Castleford in 1989, the Rovers were able to embark on a mini spending spree to boost their squad, and Keighley winger Owen Simpson was one of their targets. He had been seen playing rugby union for the army and so impressed Keighley that they bought him out of the services in June 1989. 24 tries in 31 games, including two against the Rovers in the Yorkshire Cup game in September 1989, and 8 tries in only 7 matches at the start of 1990/91, prompted Rovers to pay £50,000 for his transfer in November 1990.

He made his senior debut at home to Castleford on 11 November 1990 and scored his first try. His centre was young Paul Newlove, and this was the beginning of an exciting partnership which soon flourished. Simpson was extremely fast and proved to be one of the deadliest finishers in the game. He was the perfect partner to benefit from the space created by Newlove's presence and polished centre play. 12 tries in 23 appearances were his contribution in his first season, followed by 23 tries in 36 appearances in 1991/92. That was not enough to prevent the Rovers slipping into the Second Division, but Newlove and Simpson helped spearhead an instant return with a record-breaking 1992/93 season.

Cyril Woolford's club try-scoring record of 31 in a season had been set up in 1958/59. Both players were soon running in the tries against Second Division opposition in a league system whereby the eight clubs involved played each other four times. On 21 March 1993, Simpson was the first to pass Woolford's record with his two tries at home to Bramley, but Newlove scored the last three tries in a 60-0 victory to equal Simpson's record and then broke it in the following game. The pair scored 82 tries between them as Rovers amassed 996 points and won both the Second Division Championship as well as the Divisional Premiership Trophy.

Newlove departed in the close season of 1993 to end a partnership which had yielded 155 tries in three seasons, with Simpson contributing 69. He registered another 14 in 1993/94, when the good fortune which had enabled him to be virtually injury free and play in 118 games out of 123 since his debut, came to an end. Worse still, he was involved in an accident which deprived him of most of the following season and he only returned to play in the last five games. His last season was 1996, playing his last game appropriately enough against his former club Keighley on 28 July 1996. Although there are discrepancies in the records, it would appear that he just failed to reach his century of tries for the Rovers.

Total appearances: 155   Tries: 99   Points: 340

Tommy Smales was the one that got away initially, in that as an outstanding junior with Sharlston and Featherstone, he signed for Wigan in 1958. It didn't quite work out there and he was transferred to Barrow in 1960. Five years later, his career seemed to be going nowhere when Rovers came along and he returned to the fold. The Rovers paid £750, but what a bargain he proved to be as he enjoyed a new lease of life. He made his senior debut at Bradford on 25 September 1965. Although he did not score then, it was the beginning of a remarkable sequence. From then until 22 October 1966, he played in all 45 matches, amassing 321 points and only failing to score in two matches.

He had kicked 90 goals in his first season and as he continued his run into 1966/67, he raced to the fastest century of points for the club in only nine matches and by the end of that season, he had also scored the fastest century of goals, finishing with 122. Even more significant was his part in the historic Challenge Cup run which more than compensated for the disappointment of defeat in the Yorkshire Cup final v. Hull KR in November 1966. He kicked eight goals in the defeats of Bradford, Wakefield, Castleford and Leeds on the way to the final, where his three goals and a try against his former club, Barrow, contributed to their 17-12 defeat. His marksmanship was vital in that season, but he happily took a back seat in goal-kicking with the arrival of Cyril Kellett from Hull KR in January 1968. 10 goals in the 50-15 Yorkshire Cup defeat of York in September 1966 had been his best match goal tally, but seven goals and three tries v. Dewsbury (at home) on 16 September 1967 gave him his best points tally (23 points), a game in which he reached his 500th point for the club.

Apart from his goal-kicking, Smales was a creative loose forward and was never challenged in his career at Featherstone. After injury had restricted his appearances to 22 in 1968/69 (his lowest season's total), he made a positive start to 1969/70 with 14 successive appearances, which included another successful route to the Yorkshire Cup final. He even kicked a rare goal in the semi-final against Hull KR which with four goals from Cyril Kellett, gave his team a narrow 10-9 victory. Regrettably, Rovers miserable record in the Yorkshire Cup continued as they lost their third successive final with Hull winning 12-9. Two weeks later he played at Dewsbury and then decided to retire at the age of thirty and later turned to coaching. He succeeded Peter Fox as coach at Featherstone in the close season of 1974, but resigned in September as the job was taking up too much of his time and affecting his full-time employment.

Total appearances: 129 (+1)   Tries: 24   Goals: 269   Points: 610

Ian Smales

A wag commented that one never knew which jersey Ian Smales would appear in, which was a tribute to his versatility. Wing, centre, stand-off, second row and loose forward were all positions he occupied during his Rovers career and it was only in his last two seasons that he settled into the pack. The son of former Rovers loose forward Tommy Smales, Ian was BARLA's Player of the Year in 1987 and signed for Rovers from Lock Lane in April 1987. He played in the second row upon his debut at home to Rochdale in September 1987 but was soon alternating between backs and forwards. He scored his first try, at centre, against the Papua New Guinea touring team on 11 October 1987 and by the end of the season he was fulfilling the promise shown. Whatever position he played, his natural football ability and skills ensured his adaptability.

Ten tries in 1988/89 confirmed his try-scoring potential and he added 11 more in 1989/90. On 5 November 1989, he played at stand-off against Bradford in the Yorkshire Cup final as Rovers again suffered defeat by 20-14, but he switched back to the second row towards the end of the season. He crowned many impressive outings with a storming display in the league fixture with Bradford in April 1990, which probably clinched his selection for the 1990 Great Britain tour of Papua and New Guinea. He made seven appearances on the tour, scoring one try, and although he did not play in any of the Tests, it was an enriching experience.

His imposing progress continued in 1990/91, when he headed the club try-scoring list with 19 (playing mainly in the backs). An impressive debut for Yorkshire v. Lancashire on 18 September 1991 was crowned with his try which secured a 17-12 victory. The Rovers were in trouble however, and dropped to the Second Division at the end of the season. Smales contributed to the way back in one season as he scored his best season's total of 22 tries and 14 goals in 35 appearances. Crowned as Second Division champions, the Rovers finished the season in style, winning the Divisional Premiership Trophy against Workington by 20-16, with Smales scoring in the preliminary rounds against Ryedale York and Dewsbury. He was now back in the second row and the final was to be his last game as he was transferred to Castleford in August. His versatility in positions matched his versatility in play. He was a strong runner, quick off the mark, tackled well and was a capable touch and goal-kicker.

Total appearances: 153 (+9)   Tries: 71   Goals: 23   Points: 330

Mick Smith

Utility Back, 1964-76

positions but when coach Peter Fox arrived, he settled him at centre. Smith had the pace and flair to suit any back position, but Fox reckoned that he was primarily a finisher rather than a playmaker, and centre it was.

In a remarkably consistent career, he featured in the Yorkshire Cup finals of 1966, 1969 and 1970 and the Captain Morgan Trophy final of 1974 (all defeats, sadly), and was only one of three players to appear in the 1967, 1973 and 1974 RL Cup Finals and earn two winner's medals. He gained almost immediate television 'repeat' fame with the spectacular try he scored against Bradford in the 1973 final when his 'duck and dive' style, and his ability to side-step either way, were demonstrated to perfection as he beat five Bradford defenders to score under the posts.

He was always amongst the tries, as his career record of 115 illustrates. He topped the club try-scoring list in 1971/72 with 20, and in 1974/75, when he was given his testimonial for ten years' service, he registered two hat-tricks v. Halifax in December 1974 and Widnes in April 1975. He scored many spectacular tries and none better than his effort against Bramley (at home) on 23 March 1966, when on his own '25', he slipped his opposing number 6, straightened out to beat the full-back and then held off a three-man pursuit. The pinnacle has, however, to be the home match v. Doncaster on 13 April 1968, when from the stand-off position he scored six tries to shatter Jack Hirst's five tries in a match record which had stood since 1929 – an amazing feat, which has since been equalled by Chris Bibb in 1989.

It was in the mid-1960s that the Rovers first ventured into the Rossington junior area and made two signings – Harry Brown and Mick Smith. Brown's career was cut short by injury, but Mick Smith proved a gem and he served the club well. He was immediately thrust into the senior team in a daunting clash at Wigan on 31 October 1964. The eighteen-year-old youngster acquitted himself well and he only missed one game during the rest of the season, as well as scoring 10 tries. Signed as a stand-off, he occupied that position until 1969 when he fluctuated between wing and centre

Mick Smith was a classy player whose exciting pace made him elusive, whether he was accelerating from standing or setting off on one of his many long runs. He was always supporting and encouraging players. On 4 September 1976 he played full-back at Leeds in a 12-12 draw, his last game for the Rovers as he then transferred to Huddersfield for £500.

Total appearances: 347 (+26)　　　Tries: 115　　　Goals: 1　　　Points: 347

Peter Smith
Second Row/Loose Forward, 1973-91

The record for most appearances by a player has stood since 1934, when Jim Denton retired after 440 games. One player who might have overtaken that record total was Peter Smith, who made 419 appearances but who suffered serious injuries in the middle of his career. During that crucial period, he made only 12 appearances in three seasons which would prove to be significant. Nevertheless, there was much more to recount in Smith's career.

He was signed at the age of seventeen from the Featherstone juniors, but the Club introduced him gradually to senior football. He made his debut as a substitute *v.* Rochdale (at home) in January 1974, and made his full debut at Bramley on 14 January 1974. The Rovers embarked on their 1974 Wembley trail soon afterwards, and Smith was a substitute in the semi-final *v.* Leigh but he did not make the final. However, by October he was reintroduced and his career had begun in earnest. Indeed, from that time, he was to reign supreme for fifteen years and he came to earn the reputation of being one of the greatest forwards to play for Featherstone.

The Rovers were inching their way to the First Division Championship in the mid-1970s, finishing fourth in 1974/75 and second in 1975/76 and gathering together the pack which would provide the backbone of the bid. Farrar, Bridges, Thompson, Smith, Stone and Bell were the powerful six who helped the club to its first First Division Championship in 1976/77 and for Smith it was an outstanding season. He made 40 appearances and headed the try-scoring count with 20 – a new record for a forward, beating Willis Fawley's record of 17. At the end of the season, he was selected for the World Cup squad being played in Australasia and he made two substitute appearances against Australia in June. He made 7 appearances, on the tour scoring 2 tries. He was to make three further substitute appearances for Great Britain, but made full appearances for the Under 24s *v.* Australia in October 1978, for England *v.* France in March 1980 and finally

for Great Britain *v.* Australia at Leeds in November 1982.

It was whilst training with a Great Britain squad in 1983 that Smith was to suffer a crippling injury. He had enjoyed another successful season, culminating in his first Wembley appearance, where his experience was a vital factor in Rovers 14-12 victory over Hull. In a freak accident whilst weight training, he suffered a mystery back injury which badly affected the next three years. As a measure of how he was regarded, Great Britain coach Frank Myler selected him for the game against France at Leeds on 17 February 1984, even though he had only made one substitute appearance for his club the week before. Unfortunately, the gamble backfired and a shoulder injury put him back on the sidelines and out of the 1984 tour.

Four appearances between 1984 and 1986 must have been hard to endure, but the nightmare of injuries finally ended in February 1986, when he returned for the Cup-tie with Widnes and was able to play 10 matches before the end of the season – which brightened his testimonial year. It was back to normal service with 36 appearances in

Total appearances: 388 (+31)   Tries: 110   Drop Goals: 1   Points: 365

Peter Smith scoring against Oldham on 21 February 1988 on his way to a record career total of 110 tries by a forward.

1986/87 and 10 tries, which took him past Cliff Lambert's all-time record of 82 for tries by a forward. Relegation to the Second Division was disappointing but in another record season, Smith made a massive contribution to the swift return to the First Division, being a model of consistency. His club record of tries in a season had been broken by David Hobbs in 1982, but Smith powered in for 21 tries in 38 appearances to equal the record.

He again injured his shoulder in a pre-season friendly at Halifax in August 1989 and although he recovered to make 10 appearances, he learned after the game at Wigan on 18 November that the injury would require an operation and he decided that at the age of thirty-four and after 17 seasons, that this was the time to retire. In a fantastic career, he had shared personal and club glory with his appearances for Great Britain and England and three appearances for Yorkshire after his debut in 1978. At club level, he had savoured winners' medals in the 1983 RL Cup and the 1977 First Division, and had been runner-up in the Second Division Premiership Trophy in 1988 and the Yorkshire Cup. His record in the Yorkshire Cup is perhaps unique. He played in all three of the Rovers finals in 1976 v. Leeds, in 1977 v. Castleford and in 1989 v.

Bradford, and he had scored a try in each – and yet he finished on the losing side. He won the John Jepson Trophy as Player of the Season on a record three occasions and was voted the Second Division Player of the Year in 1988. His try-scoring and appearances speak for themselves. He came close to taking the club's appearances record, but his final try-scoring record for a forward of 110 will take some beating. It places him tenth in Rovers' all-time career try-scorers and the leading forward on the list. After a fourteen-month lay-off, he was given a free transfer in February 1991 and joined the newly-formed Scarborough Pirates as captain. He made 13 appearances and scored 2 tries, but the club folded after one season.

Such feats bear testimony to a great player, but what actually made him a great player? He was a true professional, always maintaining a high level of fitness. In attack he was a strong runner, a powerful forager and good with the ball in his hands, but it was his defensive capabilities which were truly amazing. His tackling and cover work were phenomenal. He was dedicated to the Rovers and well respected throughout the RL world as a supreme footballer and sportsman. Only a player with the stature, ability and courage of Peter Smith could have achieved so much.

Graham Steadman
Stand Off, 1986-89

Although he played his junior football in the Featherstone area, Graham Steadman actually signed for York and from 1982 to 1986 he dominated their points-scoring, with 762 points (63 tries, 253 goals, 14 drop goals). 18 of those points were scored against the Rovers when they won their Yorkshire Cup encounter at York in September 1985 by 26 points to 18. With this memory, the Rovers made a move for Steadman in February 1986, when the reported £50,000 fee was a record for both clubs – he was one of the few of the club's expensive signings to prove a great success.

Steadman was soon in business for his new club and he marked his debut at Leeds on 16 February 1986 in imposing style. Rovers lost 44-6, but Steadman scored his side's solitary try with a chip over in his own half and expert kick on to score under the posts; he also prevented three Leeds touchdowns with his strong defence. In the penultimate game of the season, he virtually repaid his transfer fee when, with six minutes remaining in the game at Halifax, he pounced on a Fox up and under to score the try which, with Quinn's conversion, drew the match 13-13, and saved Rovers from the drop into the Second Division. It was only a stay of execution though, for they were relegated at the end of the next season.

He was the ideal half-back partner for Deryck Fox and with his fantastic pace he was ever ready to supplement Fox's industry. His goal-kicking skills were not required until the departure of Steve Quinn in December 1988. Always a classy explosive impact player who had the talent to turn any game, he scored some exceptional tries and headed the try-scoring with 17 in 1987/88. His brilliant performance and two tries in the Second Division Trophy final against Oldham in May 1988 almost won the match, Rovers losing in the last minutes by 28-26. He added another 14 in 1988/89 including two superb 75-yard efforts again against Oldham in an 18-14 win in September. When Quinn retired at the end of 1988, he took up the reins and slotted over 46 goals in the remainder of that season. He had made one substitute appearance for Yorkshire when with York in 1985, and he repeated this with the Rovers in September 1988.

He flew out to play for Gold Coast Giants (Sydney) in May 1989, with his contract with the Rovers expiring in August (his last match was at Hull on 7 May 1989). With accusations of illegal approaches by a club before his contract expired, he was placed on the transfer list at a world record fee of £185,000. Castleford offered £100,000 after Steadman had agreed terms with them. The matter was referred to the Rugby League tribunal, who set the fee at £145,000 with a further £25,000 if he played for Great Britain. The deal became a then record £170,000 when he made his Test debut *v.* France at Leeds in April 1990. He had further success with Castleford and Great Britain before turning to coaching and he is currently coaching in the Super League with Castleford.

Total appearances: 95 (+1)   Tries: 48   Goals: 76   Drop Goals: 6   Points: 350

Richard 'Charlie' Stone

Forward, 1970-78 & 1983-84

I wonder if any other Rugby League player has ever handed back their signing on fee, but this is what Richard 'Charlie' Stone did in 1970. He had signed from the Old Pomfretians RU Club and made his senior debut at Wigan on 14 October 1970, impressed, and then played the next two games at home to Warrington and at Huddersfield. He then decided to quit, and handed back his signing-on fee when ironically he could have been playing in the Yorkshire Cup final two weeks hence and in only what would have been his fifth game. Fortunately, new coach Peter Fox prevailed upon him to return in the close season of 1971.

Although his three introductory games has been in the second row, Stone soon moved to loose forward at the beginning of 1971/72, a position he was to dominate before moving back into the second row in 1975/76. Initially it was sheer raw talent, but with coaching and maturity he developed into an outstanding player. Coach Peter Fox tells of how he took Stone out in training and told him to run at him and then attempt to side-step. Fox had to pick

himself up from the ground on several occasions before he had learned to side-step off one foot and the lesson was completed with a strong addition to Stone's armoury. He was exceptionally fit, which fuelled his phenomenal work rate and as his handling skills improved, his hard foraging and extraordinary defence made him a formidable opponent and a vital component in the Rovers pack. For a forward, his appearances levels were extremely high, and from 1971 to 1977, he averaged 36 appearances per season.

After appearing at loose forward in the 1973 Cup Final, he was playing substitute in both the 1974 Cup Final and the Captain Morgan Trophy final. Like most Rovers players, he could only land a runners-up medal in the Yorkshire Cup in 1976 and 1977. He made two appearances for Yorkshire in September 1973 against Cumberland and Lancashire. In 1977/78, he won the John Jepson 'Player of the Year' trophy, a just reward for his sterling performances and then followed Vince Farrar to Hull during the close season in a £15,000 transfer deal. There, he enjoyed further success, appearing in 10 finals, being appointed captain – testament to his leadership qualities – and touring Australasia in 1979 with Great Britain. He is, however, best remembered in Featherstone as the Hull player who gave away the penalty from which his former club snatched a dramatic 14-12 victory in the 1983 Cup Final.

Stone then returned to Featherstone in October 1983 to add his experience to a struggling Rovers pack through a rent-a-player scheme which Hull introduced. He played 14 games between October 1983 and February 1984, the most satisfying of which must have been the second round John Player Trophy game at home to Hull on 20 October. The Rovers had a patched-up team, with only four of their Wembley players and, in an ironic twist, Stone inspired them to a 20-14 victory over the league champions. He allegedly retired after playing at Leigh on 24 February 1984, but he joined Bradford Northern for one last season in 1984/85 with a creditable 28 appearances – a striking finish to a striking career.

Total appearances: 241 (+21)   Tries: 26   Points: 79

Billy Stott
Stand Off/Centre, 1930-33

Billy Stott gained fame as the first winner of the Lance Todd Trophy for Man of the Match in the RL Cup Final. Captaining Wakefield Trinity against Wigan in 1946, he scored two tries and two goals, his second goal giving Trinity a dramatic 13-12 victory in the closing stages. Most of Featherstone applauded this feat as Stott was Featherstone born and bred and had commenced his rugby league career with the Rovers.

He was signed from Featherstone juniors on his seventeenth birthday, having played two trial matches in the senior team at stand-off under an assumed name of 'Owens'. At that time, the Rovers did not have a reserve team and it was straight into the senior team, but he had tremendous talent despite his youth, and he scored 2 tries and 11 goals in his 9 appearances. He sparkled in the following season with a positive maturity despite the club's lowly league position with 37 appearances and had a personal best match total of 10 points (two tries and two goals) v. Bradford (at home) in April 1931. With Jim Denton still around he was, however, only the occasional goal-kicker.

His stylish play soon established him as a future star and in 1932 he moved to centre to accommodate Wilf Evans, and underlying his natural talent and skills was even more productive. As the Rovers sank to third from the bottom, he was the shining star in a dismal season and the inevitable question arose as to whether the club would be able to hang on to such talent. The answer was swift. After only four games in the following season, he played what was to be his last game at Batley on 9 September 1933. The following week he was selected to play for Yorkshire v. Australia at Headingley and on that day he was transferred to Broughton Rangers for £750 – a huge amount in those days and again Rovers had had to sell a star so that the club could survive. What is not clear is whether Stott signed before or after the county match, and whether he should be listed as another Rovers county player!

He played with Broughton, then moved to Oldham and was transferred to Wakefield in 1945 for £95. In an illustrious career, he played in 502 games, scoring 163 tries and 589 goals, a total of 1,667 points. He made seven appearances for Yorkshire from 1933 to 1938 and made one appearance for England v. Wales at Pontypridd in November 1936. Of his many fine displays for Featherstone, his talent is perhaps best personified in the Rovers v. Huddersfield game on 11 April 1933. Star-studded Huddersfield were RL Cup finalists and had won 12 of their last 13 games. Featherstone were lying at the bottom of the league with only six victories. In an amazing game which was dominated by Stott, the Rovers were only losing 8-7 with one minute to go. With one last effort, Stott received the ball on the half-way line, kicked through and speedily followed up to regain possession. One of his famous swerves took him past two defenders and as the full-back confronted him, Stott took him over the line as he scored the winning try. The crowd erupted and Stott was chaired from the field.

Total appearances: 103   Tries: 27   Goals: 63   Points: 207

Arthur Street
Loose Forward, 1940-46

During the Second World War, rugby league was organised in War Emergency Leagues and whilst some clubs had difficulties in maintaining fixtures, Featherstone was one club which endeavoured to play its full part. They were fortunate in that with most of their players exempt from military service through working in the local collieries, they were able to preserve the nucleus of the team and continue to develop young players. Arthur Street was one such player who signed from Glasshoughton Juniors in 1940 and made his debut at Hull on 9 November 1940 at the age of eighteen. When he joined the club, he was a hot-headed youngster, but he developed into a constructive loose forward who could read a game shrewdly.

During the war years, he played regularly for the Rovers and enjoyed his best season in 1942/43 when he not only played in every game, but finished as leading try and points scorer with 8 tries and 24 points (only 23 league and cup games were played, with Rovers winning 10 games). This included his only hat-trick of tries scored in the 36-8 victory at home to York in March 1943. His brother Bill also played for the Rovers from 1942, as a utility back and they played 12 matches together before Arthur's form attracted the attention of Dewsbury, who were a power in the game in the immediate post-war years. Street played against them on 25 October 1946 at Post Office Road and, three weeks later, he was transferred there for £350 – and the Rovers eternal cycle of financial problems was temporarily eased.

He made 126 appearances for Dewsbury, and was described as the best forward on the field when they lost 13-4 to Wigan in the League Championship final of 1947. Wigan scored eight of their points whilst Street was off the field having his ear stitched. His younger brother Harry joined him in 1948 and he was to have an illustrious career with Dewsbury, Wigan and England before ending his days with a brief spell at Featherstone. Arthur transferred to Doncaster in 1951 to spearhead the new club's entry into rugby league and he was the mainstay of the team as he made 40 appearances in that first season. A brief spell at Wakefield followed in 1953 when he retired. He then returned to his first love, Featherstone Rovers, when he took up coaching and he had a successful partnership as 'A' team coach with Harold Moxon from 1957 to 1963. His knowledge of the game was vast and he had the satisfaction of coaching the 'A' team to the Yorkshire Senior Competition Championship in 1961/62, when future stars Carl Dooler, Ivor Lingard, Arnie Morgan, Les Tonks, Terry Ramshaw and Keith Cotton emerged. He also served on the club committee.

Total appearances: 106   Tries: 25   Points: 75

Alan Tennant
Centre, 1948-59

A member of another famous Featherstone footballing family, Alan's father played for Hull KR and his brothers Walt and Nelson for the Rovers. He had captained a very successful intermediate side and scored 46 tries in 1947/48, after which he was pursued by many clubs but chose to trial with the Rovers. Given his family background, it is not surprising that his preference lay with his home-town club.

He played his first game on the wing under the name of 'Jackson' at Dewsbury on 25 December 1948, with his brother Walt as centre. He scored a try and repeated the act at home against Castleford in the Boxing Day encounter, and he was then signed for what was reported to be the highest fee paid for a junior player.

He was back in his preferred position of centre in 1949/50 and benefited from a brief partnership with Don Graham, the Australian centre who inspired Rovers in early 1950 and described Tennant as one of the most promising three-quarters in the game. National Service intervened, but Tennant established himself upon his return and launched into one of his most successful seasons in 1951/52 with 41 appearances (missing only four games). He was a vital member of the 1952 side culminating in the historic visit to Wembley in April 1952. Although not a regular try-scorer, his two tries at home to Castleford in December 1951 won the game 15-10 for Rovers, an important victory as Rovers struggled in the league despite their Cup success.

Although he was the most consistent player in 1953/54 with 37 appearances, he lost his regular place shortly afterwards but, typically, was content to lend his experience to the 'A' team and yet be available when necessary for senior team duty. He enjoyed spells between 1956 and 1958 and was a member of the team which performed heroics in the 1958 Challenge Cup, including the famous 5-0 defeat of St Helens before losing out in the semi-final to Workington. He also re-appeared against the Australians in November 1959,

when he scored in the convincing 23-15 victory, but at the end of that season he decided to retire. The club had granted him a testimonial in 1958/59 and the tribute he earned from the local *Express* summed up his career so aptly: 'His career was like a beacon. After Wembley at twenty-one, he accepted 'A' team football three years later with an enthusiasm which did him great credit. His example did much for inexperienced youngsters, and all the time he was fit and ready to answer the call for the senior team. He was the rugged, rather than the classic centre, hampered from reaching the heights because his pace never matched his undoubted strength. Defence was his main feature and he has marked and floored the best.' At his peak, his forceful bursts down the centre and his weaving runs were likened to his brother Walt and few could surpass his consistent tackling and close marking. Above all, he typified the ideal club man.

Total appearances: 214   Tries: 41   Points: 123

through, beating two men, and as he streaked for the corner he timed his reverse pass to Longley to perfection for the winger to score – an early example of his artistry.

With peace-time football resuming in 1945, he again headed the try-scoring lists with 16 tries and continued to add to his blossoming talent. Against the formidable Bradford Northern side, he was the best tackler on the field in a creditable 5-5 draw, preventing both Kitching and Batten from scoring with incredible tackles. At York in December, he scored a hat-trick and for his third try he beat the opposing wingman and raced 70 yards to score. Rovers lost 21-11 and Tennant later recalled that it must have been unique to have scored six hat-tricks in his career and finish on the losing side in four of the matches.

In 1946, dissatisfied with playing on the wing, he asked for a transfer and joined Wakefield for £700 in March. It must have been the shortest transfer on record because he rejoined Rovers in January 1947. He continued to excel and yet another of many examples of his sheer talent was at home to Hunslet in November 1948 when, having saved a try with a tackle on Bowman, he received the ball from Allman in his own half, ran strongly and straight, and then pretended to kick and hoodwinked Griffiths, the Hunslet full-back, to speed under the posts with several in pursuit. Appointed captain in January 1949, he then made his Yorkshire county debut *v.* Cumberland at Workington on 6 April 1949. A broken finger deprived him of a second appearance against Lancashire as well as the opportunity of breaking his own try-scoring record – he had scored 15 in 27 appearances.

There was no more inspiring sight in the Rovers' dismal post-war record in the late 1940s than that of Walt Tennant either streaking across to score a try or pulling off a try-saving tackle. He was a class centre and made his senior debut at home to Warrington on 30 August 1939, three days before war was declared. He had graduated from Girnhill Intermediates, where he played centre with Jack Blackburn. The War Emergency Leagues were introduced from 1939 to 1945, and Tennant relished the opening two seasons with 18 tries in 34 appearances in 1939/40 and 19 tries in 22 appearances in 1940/41; he headed the try-scoring lists on both occasions and helped Rovers to a respectable mid-table position. The highlight of that first season was his Yorkshire Cup final medal when Rovers beat Wakefield Trinity 12-9 in June 1940 and Tennant was outstanding. He scored the first try and then engineered the second. He cut

He was granted a testimonial in September 1950, which concluded in May 1951 by which time he had decided to retire. Although only thirty, the major role he had taken in both defence and attack in twelve seasons had taken its toll – but what memories he left behind! He was also proud of the fact that he never appeared in the reserves throughout his whole career.

Total appearances: 234   Tries: 104   Goals: 2   Points: 314

Vaughan Thomas
Winger, 1963-68

Yet another product of the famous Sharlston nursery, Vaughan Thomas played his junior football with Wakefield Trinity but was invited to attend training at Post Office Road by Willis Fawley, the Rovers hooker, and signed in October 1963. He got his chance later that season after some sound displays in the reserves and he scored on his debut, at home to Huddersfield, as Rovers won 23-3. Indeed, he finished the season in style, scoring 7 tries in 11 appearances.

More impressive form in 1964/65 led to his selection for the Great Britain Under 24 team *v.* France at Oldham in October 1965 and with 32 appearances for Rovers he only missed six games during the season. He started 1966/67 with a bang when he went in for his only hat-trick of tries at home to York in the first round Yorkshire Cup victory by 50-15. There were hopes of a first Winners medal in the Yorkshire Cup final *v.* Hull KR on 15 October 1966, but a substandard performance by Rovers saw them lose 25-12, with Thomas hardly touching the ball. By the start of the RL Cup campaign in February, coach Laurie Gant had increased his options amongst the backs with the return of Jordan and the acquisition of Newlove. Thomas played in the rounds against Bradford and Castleford, but missed out against Wakefield and against Leeds in the semi-final. He resumed to play in the last four league games and did sufficiently well to convince coach Laurie Gant that he should play at Wembley – although the decision was made so late that he was not even included in the Wembley programme! He more than justified his selection, however, and he had his moment of glory when he sped in to pick up a spilled ball early in the second half and score one of the tries that sealed Barrow's fate.

After a promising start to 1967/68, he was briefly transfer-listed in November but then announced in February 1968 that he was retiring from football. He was transfer-listed again at £3,500 and then signed for Bradford Northern. Sadly, a knee injury caused him to retire permanently from the game in September 1969.

A cousin of Carl Dooler, Thomas was a very talented winger. His high stepping action was different, but with his pace and strength he had the ability to take his chances, particularly with his no-nonsense running style. Similarly, his tackling was unorthodox but very effective. He was very fit and a quick thinker and it was a pity that his football career should end so comparatively early. His last game for Featherstone was at home to Widnes on 6 January 1968.

Total appearances: 108   Tries: 35   Points: 105

Jimmy Thompson
Second Row/Prop Forward, 1966-77

Introduced by chance to rugby league at sixteen, a young junior in his first match was so unfamiliar with the game that he punched the ball when it was kicked to him from the kick-off. That same youngster then learned so quickly that he was soon selected for Yorkshire Under 17s. The coach was due to leave Leeds for Lancashire at 7.30 a.m. and because he had no money, he walked fifteen miles from Knottingley to Leeds to catch the bus. That youngster was Jimmy Thompson, and his subsequent analysis of the 'punching' incident was that 'he might not have understood the game in those early days, but even then nobody got past him'. These anecdotes perfectly illustrate why Jimmy Thompson's attitude and determination made him the RL star that he was, despite having to overcome some devastating injuries.

After that interesting start, he signed from the Rovers juniors in June 1966 and, initially, made a substitute appearance at home to Hull KR on 1 October 1966, before making a full appearance at Leigh the following week. He did not play in Rovers' Yorkshire Cup final on 15 October, but was reinstated in the team after the final. Despite his inexperience and youth, he

dedicated himself to a high level of fitness and he developed his skills in a manner which almost bordered on the fanatical, but his dedication yielded results. Initially, he couldn't even pass properly and Keith Goulding spent hours on the training field making him pass the ball to hit the posts – and another facet of his game was complete. He applied himself to everything and even his play the ball technique was well nigh perfect!

The capabilities of the young Thompson were vividly illustrated in that first season. His inclusion in the 1967 RL Cup team with its tough encounters all the way to the final against premier Yorkshire club opposition demanded a high level of defensive work which he revelled in. His tackling stint in the final was remarkable for an eighteen year old and his tackle on Murray snuffed out a Barrow try. Equally, it was his run from half-way, only to be downed by Tees two yards from the line, which led to Arnie Morgan scoring from the resultant play.

From that impressive first season he became better and better, despite lengthy lay-offs through serious injuries. He was incapacitated from August 1971 to November 1972, October 1973 to April 1974 and November 1974 to August 1975, and at one stage understandably thought his career was over. He owed his resurrection to the surgical skills of Mr Bain at Durham.

In the midst of these injuries was interwoven an amazing success story. At club level, after collecting his winner's medal against Barrow, he became one of only three Featherstone players to appear in all three finals of 1967, 1973 and 1974. It was a close thing for the 1974 final against Warrington. He had been out through injury from October 1973 and missed all the rounds including the semi-final v. Leigh on 30 March. He returned on 3 April to play in six of the last seven league games and prove his fitness. Further club honours were runners-up medals in the Yorkshire Cup finals of 1969 and 1970, but he missed the 1976 final because of injury. The pinnacle then was the First Division Championship in 1976/77. When Thompson returned to full fitness at the beginning of

---

Total appearances: 270 (+12)   Tries: 41   Points: 123

A young Jimmy Thompson tussles with Sid Hynes (Leeds).

1975/76, he switched to prop a position he had 'acquired' successfully at international level. He only missed one game that season with 38 appearances and he became part of what was probably the most successful front row in the club's history – Thompson, Bridges and Farrar. The Rovers finished runners-up, but in 1976/77 they succeeded in landing the league title for the only time in their history – and Thompson weighed in with another mammoth appearances total of 37 out of 41 matches, earning him the John Jepson Trophy for Player of the Season. Although not renowned for his try-scoring, he did score a hat-trick at home to Workington in April 1971.

His impressive representative career commenced on 17 April 1969, when he played for Great Britain v. France in the Under 24 game at Castleford. Six months later, he earned his county debut for Yorkshire v. Cumberland at Hull, the first of 11 appearances during which he captained the side in 1971. His selection for the Great Britain tour of Australasia in 1970 led to his full international debut, when he played in the Second Test v. Australia in Sydney on 20 June 1970. Great Britain had lost the First Test and Thompson replaced Don Robinson. The pack of Hartley Fisher, Watson, Laughton, Thompson and Reilly was the best he ever played in and laid the foundation for Great Britain's 28-7 victory in the Second Test, and 21-17 in the Third Test. That was the last time that the Ashes were won by Great Britain. The two Tests against New Zealand were also won and, in a very crowded international year, Thompson then played in the World Cup held in England in the autumn. Although disrupted by injury, Thompson was firmly established on the international scene and he toured Australasia again in 1974 [when he played in 21 of 28 games, was rated one of the successes, and appeared (successfully) in the prop position for the first time to help the tour manager out] and in 1977 with another World Cup tournament.

When he returned home in June 1977, his well-earned testimonial season had been concluded and two months later he was transferred to Bradford Northern for £10,000, where he was reunited with former coach Peter Fox. He, as much as anyone, was fully aware of Thompson's worth and he gave great service to that club before finally moving for a final season with the newly formed Carlisle in 1981/82. He played in 21 games, but then dislocated his shoulder and decided to retire.

Jimmy Thompson is a marvellous example for any aspiring sportsman. He took to the rugby league game with raw natural ability, but it was his dedication, application, determination and aptitude which shaped his illustrious career. Renowned for his defensive work, his copy-book tackling was awesome. His work rate was exceptional and his fearless and competitive approach was exemplary. He set the standards to inspire others.

Known as the 'Gentle Giant', Les Tonks was a colossus of a man who was 6ft 3in tall and weighed 18.5st; he played a more important part in the Rovers team than outsiders credited. He was signed from the junior side in June 1960 and was given time to gain experience in the reserves. His first appearance for the seniors was at Warrington on 9 September 1961 but that was only one of two appearances he made that season, as he was mainly involved in helping the 'A' team win the Yorkshire Senior Competition Championship. With Abe Terry, Len Hammill and Malcolm Dixon competing for the prop positions, his appearances continued to be restricted and what a tough baptism he had. After his appearance at Warrington, his next appearances were at Doncaster, Wakefield, Huddersfield, Swinton and Halifax before he finally made his home debut v. Hull KR in April 1963.

With the departure of Hammill and Terry,

he was able to establish himself from 1964, but missed out on a Yorkshire Cup final medal in November 1966 with the arrival of Colin Forsyth. They vied for the number 8 position as the Rovers embarked on their 1967 Wembley run, but Tonks won the day and made the first of three appearances for Rovers at Wembley. He is one of only three players who played in 1967, 1973 and 1974. He also made the Yorkshire Cup final team which lost to Hull in November 1969 but, again, he missed out in the 1970 encounter with Leeds. Indeed, his career might have taken a different turn then because he went on loan to Hull KR in 1970 but declined to move permanently and was then back in favour at the beginning of 1970/71. From then, he was a model of consistency, enjoying a run of 43 consecutive appearances from September 1971 to October 1972 and, when that was broken, he promptly embarked on another consecutive run of 50 appearances from February 1973 to March 1974, when he was injured at Rochdale. In the midst of this consistency, he earned the Player of the Year award for 1972/73, the same season appropriately enough, which had been designated for his testimonial. 40 appearances in both 1972 and 1973 were fitting testimony to his consistency and stamina, but when coach Peter Fox moved to Wakefield during the close season of 1974, he decided to join Fox there. His last match was, therefore, the 1974 RL Cup final against Warrington, when he gained his only Wembley runners-up medal.

Tonks was top class in the days when prop forwards were vital in providing solidity in the pack and enabling the hooker to pivot successfully to strike for the ball. His stature was deceptive as he seemingly ambled through a game, but he read the game shrewdly and often appeared at the right place at the right time. He was a committed advocate of moving up the middle of the field having passed the ball, because the ball would invariably come back to the middle. He was always encouraging younger players in his quiet unassuming way, but no-one bossed the pack when he was around – a gentle giant indeed!

Total appearances: 285 (+22)   Tries: 15   Goals: 1   Points: 47

Brendon Tuuta
Loose Forward, 1990-1995 & 1999

The New Zealand touring team played at Post Office Road on 7 November 1989 and won comfortably 44-20; amongst the players who impressed was loose forward Brendon Tuuta. In less than a year, he was making his Rovers debut at home to Hull KR in the second round of the Yorkshire Cup after his transfer had been negotiated from the Western Suburbs club in Australia. He was an instant success and over the next five seasons endeared himself to the Rovers. Originally, he came on a short-term contract and he was due to return to Western Suburbs early in 1991, but the Rovers bought out his contract.

Originating from the South Pacific island of Chatan, he had played for the Kiwis against Australia early in 1991 and had earned himself the nickname of 'baby-faced assassin', referring to his almost cherubic features and his no-nonsense style of play. He was tough and strong and undoubtedly played above his weight (5ft 10in, 13st 4lb), but his hard-running and ferocious tackling made him a most formidable opponent – and the crowds loved him. Off the field, he was quiet and unassuming!

He was a hard working and committed professional who was always in the thick of the action. He gave no quarter and asked for none. When Rovers were relegated in 1992/93, he was to the fore as they were immediately crowned Second Division champions and also won the Divisional Premiership Trophy final, beating Workington 20-16. One particular incident during that season demonstrated the esteem in which he was held. On 7 October 1992, he was sent off in the Yorkshire Cup game at Wakefield for an alleged high tackle on Jones, the Wakefield winger. He claimed that the tackle was innocuous, but he was suspended for two matches. Still protesting his innocence, and supported by Jones, he appealed and the suspension was raised to three matches. Outrage followed, and the club forwarded sixty letters it had received protesting over the injustice to RL headquarters, but to no avail. It was an unprecedented reaction from the fans.

When his contract ended in 1995, he moved on to play Super League football with Castleford and Warrington, but when he retired from Super League in 1999, the Rovers were happy to welcome him back and he played for one more season. The fire and determination were still unquenched and he played in 24 games. He would have played in more but his arrival from New Zealand was delayed as he caught chicken pox from his children!

This popular player certainly has a special place at Featherstone, where his whole-hearted efforts were an inspiration to the other players. Whilst his tackling and commitment were awesome, behind the ferocity was a very talented footballer who had an eye for the opening, could split defences with astute passes and displayed some very silky skills. His return for one final year with the Rovers demonstrated that the admiration and affection extended both ways!

Total appearances: 170 (+7)   Tries: 32   Drop Goals: 1   Points: 129

Gary Waterworth
Winger, 1961-64

F ew players can have made such an impressive introduction to rugby league than Gary Waterworth, who burst onto the scene in 1961. He had been playing rugby union at Roundhay and was recommended to Featherstone by Ken Baxter, a Rovers scout. It was arranged that Waterworth would have trials in the 'A' team, the first of which was at Bramley in the opening game of the season. On that eventful Friday night, he scored two brilliant tries which caused the Rovers officials to go into a hurried conference and offer terms immediately after the match. He signed, and was put straight into the senior team at home to Dewsbury on 30 August 1961. What a debut! He roused the crowd with a dazzling hat-trick. For his third try he received the ball 40 yards out and in a curving run to the corner flag he outpaced the Dewsbury defence to earn a great ovation from players and crowd alike.

Such was his rise to fame that six weeks later he made his Yorkshire county debut *v*.

Lancashire at Leigh on 9 October and he was then selected as reserve winger for the Great Britain side against the New Zealanders. In 27 games, he scored 20 tries and everyone looked to him to set a new club try-scoring record in his first season. It was then, however, that he experienced the full twist of football fate when he pulled a thigh muscle in the cup game with Leigh in March 1962 and he was out for the rest of the season. His absence in the RL Cup and League Championship semi-finals against Wakefield was a big blow.

Raring to go at the beginning of the next season, he lost the tip of one of his fingers in an accident which delayed his return until 20 October. Immediately, he showed that he had lost none of his verve and the 27-27 drawn game at Wakefield two weeks later was one of his best ever games. He created the opening for the first try by Greatorex and in the second half, he scored one of the best of his many brilliant tries. From the half-way line he beat his opposing winger and full-back in a perfectly executed run to score under the posts. Rather surprisingly, he later confided that he always felt uncomfortable on the wing and preferred centre!

He started his third season, 1963/64, with another typical burst and he registered five tries in the opening five games. Unfortunately, injury again intervened and he had to miss the Yorkshire Cup final against Halifax. Although he resumed, a shoulder injury at Warrington in April 1964 again disrupted his progress. It did not improve and in November 1964 he decided to retire after only three years. Having been injury free throughout his rugby union career, it was unfortunate that he should suffer so many on turning professional. It deprived the game of a remarkable talent which became evident in a very short period and which could have established him as a great star. His blistering pace was his main asset, but, unlike other fliers, he did not hesitate or ease up when confronted by massing defenders. No wonder coach Harold Moxon described him as the fastest finisher he had ever seen at Featherstone.

Total appearances: 68   Tries: 33   Points: 99

Ken Welburn
Prop Forward, 1947-58

The Rovers knew that they had signed an outstanding player when local youngster Ken Welburn joined them in August 1947. He was only eighteen, but he had been an impressive Featherstone junior, playing for both Yorkshire and England. With the rigorous demands on prop forwards in those days, it was decided to groom him gradually in the reserves and it was not until 20 November 1948 that he made his senior debut at Hull. His great mentor was Frank Hemingway, who wore the number 8 jersey with distinction from 1934 and it was only when he retired in 1950 that Ken took over his mantle.

He soon made his presence felt in the pack, as Arthur Wood, Bill Bradshaw and Willis Fawley will testify. As the Rovers hookers, they knew what an asset Welburn was and how dependable his scrummaging techniques were. He was a regular choice, but unfortunately his career was marred with a series of injuries – a broken ankle, broken ribs, torn ligaments, a dislocated elbow and bone grafting on his fingers. Naturally, these disrupted his career and at times had a demoralising effect but he relentlessly continued his career.

He was involved in three RL Cup runs, two of which in 1955 and 1958 both ended at the semi-final stage with defeats by Workington. In 1952, it was also Workington who thwarted the Rovers' bid to win their first RL Cup final, but despite being disappointed, he had the satisfaction of being the 'anchor' of the pack which provided the basis of the road to Wembley.

Try-scoring was not a feature of Welburn's game, but being captain in 1954/55 must have inspired him. One of his best games was against Hunslet at Featherstone on 12 March 1955, when the Rovers pulled off a surprise 18-12 win, and he contributed with two tries to play a real captain's part. He was a good captain, well respected with his quiet manner and, of course, he knew the game intimately. Typically he asked to be relieved of the captaincy in 1955/56 because he 'considered that someone in the backs who could see all the play was better equipped for the captain's role than he was'. He did, however, agree to carry on as vice-captain! He scored only 12 tries in his career, with just one on opponents' grounds – at Leeds on 16 April 1956.

He earned a well-deserved testimonial in 1957, but decided to retire at the end of the 1957/58 season. Two years later, he attempted a comeback but the old injury bug reared its head again and having sustained a knee injury in pre-season training, he decided to take the message and went back into retirement.

He was an outstanding prop of his era, even though he never won representative honours at senior level. Apart from his scrummaging skills, he was exceptionally nimble despite his bulk and his darts from the rucks would often carry him clear to create space for his colleagues.

Total appearances: 263　　　Tries: 12　　　Points: 36

Jimmy Williams
Stand Off/Scrum-Half, 1921-29

Jimmy Williams had the distinction of scoring the first points for the club in their historic opening fixture in senior football following their admission to the Northern Rugby League in June 1921. At Bradford on 27 August 1921, he received the ball on the half-way line after two minutes' play and coolly dropped a goal. A try and two more goals were a healthy contribution to a 17-3 victory. He had signed for the highly successful Featherstone junior team in 1919 and had such natural football ability that he adapted to senior football immediately, and was one of the stars who helped establish the club in the 1920s.

He made the most appearances, 37, in that opening season and was second in the points-scoring lists. Whilst Jim Denton dominated the goal and points scoring throughout that period, Williams was a very capable second-choice kicker – but he did not get many chances. He was also adept at drop goals. His best efforts were four goals and one try v. Keighley (at home) in March 1927 and five goals v. Huddersfield (at home) in September 1927. In that season, the

Rovers finished third in the league table, their highest position, and Williams combined with Jack Hirst to create the first try in Rovers impressive 15-12 Championship semi-final win at Leeds in April 1928. In the RL Cup, his try at Batley, three-time Northern Union Cup winners, in the first round in February 1922, gave the Rovers a 5-3 victory and was the first of their many legendary cup shocks. A year later, there was almost another cup shock when he excelled in the Rovers' narrow second round defeat by Wigan.

He was talented enough to have gained representative honours but, on his own admission, reckoned that players like Jonty Parkin (Wakefield) and Frank Todd (Halifax) 'took some knocking out'. His whole-hearted displays were well illustrated in his nippy breaks and the vigour he displayed. He knew the value of planned moves and was forever trying something new in his attempts to deceive the opposition. The match report of the Widnes game in November 1926 summed up his contribution – 'Williams varied his tactics very skilfully, and his cross kicks and wide passes played a great part in victory'.

After the disappointment of losing the League Championship final against Swinton in May 1928, there was further disappointment in the 1928 Yorkshire Cup. His two goals and Jack Hirst's memorable try earned a dramatic 7-4 victory at Huddersfield in the second round, and he was then prominent in the semi-final defeat of Castleford. Unfortunately, a broken nose against St Helens Recs in the next match destroyed his Cup Final dreams, although Rovers lost to Leeds 5-0.

He was granted a joint testimonial with Arthur Haigh in 1929. In those days, a match was allocated. They chose the Bradford game in April and although Rovers won 40-15, and Jack Hirst scored a record five tries, the receipts were only £14! (He eventually received £87.) This was his last game and he played on the wing. In August 1929 he was transferred to York, but was transfer-listed there in November. From 1936 to 1938, he was trainer to the Newcastle RL Club during its brief existence.

Total appearances: 211   Tries: 30   Goals: 120   Points: 330

Arthur Wood

Hooker, 1947-51

Arthur Wood was an old-fashioned hooker at a time in the game when hooking was a true speciality – and he was good at it! He signed for the club in October 1947 from Streethouse, having played in the Yorkshire amateur side v. Cumberland, and he made his debut in the RL Cup-tie at Leigh on 14 February 1948. He made 11 appearances that season, and 16 the following season and it was not until 1949/50 that he was firmly established in the senior team and showing his skill at number 9. Although the Rovers were in the lower rungs of the league table, Wood ensured that they had more than their share of possession, and he played in 40 of the 41 games that season. At home to Bramley on 4 February 1950, he scored his solitary try for the club.

At that time, Joe Egan (Wigan) was the England hooker and Len Marson (Wakefield) was his contender. As Wood's prowess and reputation grew, he was selected to play for Yorkshire v. Lancashire at Huddersfield on 18 October 1950, when Marson had to withdraw. Yorkshire won 23-15 and Wood took the scrums 21-19 against Joe Egan. His rivalry with Marson was resumed in the league fixture with Wakefield on 2 December 1950, when Wood took the scrums 15-13 in the first half, and only lost 18-15 in the second when Rovers were down to a five-man pack. These were impressive achievements and he was named reserve hooker for the England v. France game.

Such success inevitably raised the question of whether the Rovers could now hang on to their prize asset. In January 1951 in the home game with Bramley, the club took the unprecedented step of announcing on the public tannoy that 'Wood did not wish to leave Featherstone. He was very happy and it was hoped that England's potential hooker would be with us for years to come'. One part of the prophecy in that announcement soon materialised when Wood was selected to play for England v. Other Nationalities at Wigan on 11 April 1951 – Rovers' first international since Tommy Askin in 1928. One month

later, he was transferred to Leeds for £3,000, a record fee for Rovers and the highest fee paid by Leeds for a forward. It was stressed that the decision had been left to the player as he was not on the transfer list.

With Leeds, he played five more games for Yorkshire. There can be no doubt that he was an excellent hooker, but he also worked tirelessly in the loose. With his distinctive ginger hair and his heavily shin-padded legs, he was surprisingly deceptive with his running – but he didn't score many tries. Off the field, he never wore a collar and tie – just a characteristic 'muffler'.

Total appearances: 105   Tries: 1   Points: 3

Winger, 1955-61

Yet another of the famous Rovers 'bargain buys', Cyril Woolford was acquired from Doncaster in April 1956 for £400. He had commenced his senior career from Lock Lane juniors with Castleford in 1947 and he then moved to Doncaster in 1953. His positions had fluctuated between wing, centre and stand-off but at Featherstone, he made his debut on the wing v. Leeds (at home) on 7 April 1956. He scored two tries, racing 50 yards to score one of them, and the pattern was set. In six seasons he thrilled the crowds with his positive play and scored a few more tries along the way.

At the start of his next season, he switched to centre where he was even more effective. In the Yorkshire Cup-tie at Hull in September, he scored one of his finest tries when he followed up a Fox kick at great speed, racing fifty yards to touch down under Bowman's nose and win the match 7-6. He scored 8 tries that season in 27 appearances before he moved on to his purple patch from 1957. In September his displays earned him his county debut v. Lancashire at Widnes, with Yorkshire winning 25-11 and Woolford at centre. However, as the 1958 Rugby League Cup campaign got under way, he

moved back to the wing and there he would remain for the rest of his career. He played his part in those marvellous RL Cup runs of 1958, 1959, 1960 and 1961. Against St Helens (at home) in 1959, in a repeat of the previous year's encounter when Rovers won 5-0 in the snow, he scored the first try and completely bottled up Van Vollenhoven, the Saints winger, to set Rovers on another famous victory. The lone try he scored against Hull in the semi-final was the first ever scored by a Rovers player at that stage of the competition. Yet his dream of Wembley was to elude him at that last stage in three successive years, with the cruellest blow reserved for his last season. Then the controversial decision at Hull in the third round put Rovers out at a time when they had their strongest team.

Having missed only 5 of Rovers' 41 games in 1957/58, Woolford then progressed to his best season in 1958/59. He seemed to thrive from another long run of appearances (38), and his characteristic and devastating forays down the left flank drew favourable comparison with Eric Batten. He equalled Batten's club try-scoring record of 26 in a season with two tries at Wakefield on 31 March 1959, and the record became his when he scored v. Dewsbury (at home) on 4 April. He finished the season with 31 tries to set up a record which was only broken by Owen Simpson and Paul Newlove in 1992/93, when Rovers were in the Second Division and playing in a league formula which restricted the quality of the opposition. Unsurprisingly, he was voted the Player of the Season.

He then went on to further heights in 1959/60. Appointed vice-captain, he gained some recompense with a Yorkshire Cup Winners medal as Rovers avenged their RL Cup defeat with a 15-14 win over Hull – and another try from Woolford. It was his 61st for the club, breaking another of Batten's post-war record total of 60. Another appearance for Yorkshire followed, this time on the wing, when he scored in their 38-28 victory over Lancashire at Leigh on 11 November 1959. The Rovers played the Australians on that day and that was the only

Total appearances: 185   Tries: 88   Points: 264

A game to remember. Cyril Woolford watches Wyn Jones and Willis Fawley wrap up Saints' Huddart in the snow affected third round RL Cup-tie with St Helens on 8 March 1958 – Rovers won 5-0.

fixture he missed that season as he set up a club record of 46 appearances in a season – a record which still stands. Indeed, if that fixture against the Australians is ignored, Woolford had a run of 56 consecutive league and cup games from 28 March 1959, until he was injured in the opening game of 1960/61 and had to miss the Swinton game on 20 August 1960.

He took the decision to retire at the end of 1960/61 and he made his final appearance in the home game v. Batley on 19 April 1961, where a most appreciative crowd was able to pay its own tribute for what he had accomplished at Featherstone. He did not score on that occasion, but what a legacy he left – 88 tries in 185 appearances over a period of six years during which he only missed 32 games. He scored two hat-tricks, but his best tally was four tries at Dewsbury on 31 January 1959, when Rovers won 24-0 and a mis-directed pass deprived him of a fifth try which would have equalled Jack Hirst's record in a match.

He once maintained, in his advice to future players, 'that a player should never hesitate or be afraid but should go straight in, whether in attack or defence. A player's biggest asset can be speed and in tackling an opponent, precise judgement is essential and one should always go "down below" to ensure that the opponent will not elude the grasp'. This advice actually epitomises his own play. It was Woolford's whole attitude to the game which made him such an outstanding player. His will to win and eagerness to be in the action generated his enthusiasm and spawned his tenacity in defence and forcefulness in attack. It gained him esteem and respect throughout his career which extended well beyond Featherstone. On his first return to Doncaster with Featherstone, a tribute appeared in the programme as follows: 'Our thanks for the many hours of enjoyment and excitement you provided for us. Always like to see this whole-hearted player showing his paces both in attack and defence.'

Brian Wrigglesworth was one of those solid dependable players who loved and gave great service to the game. He had signed for Doncaster in 1957 from Allerton Bywater juniors and transferred to Bramley in 1958 where he remained for seven years during which he represented Yorkshire on two occasions. In 1965 he moved to Hull KR, but within a year he had transferred to Featherstone.

Although he had mainly featured at stand-off, it was at centre that he made his debut for Rovers at Hull on 29 August 1966. He was immediately involved in the Yorkshire Cup competition and six weeks later was playing against his previous club, Hull KR, in the final. Featherstone lost 25-12, but Brian Wrigglesworth earned praise as he scored his try and never conceded defeat until the end.

Rovers were having problems with the full-back position that season and on the eve of the RL Cup competition coach Laurie Gant decided to move Wrigglesworth there. It suited him perfectly. Always an adventurous player, it gave him the scope and space to expand his ebullient style. In the second-round encounter v. Cup favourites Wakefield (at home), the Rovers were losing 5-3 when Wrigglesworth moved up in support of Smales, kicked through and beat Metcalfe to the touchdown to put his team in front for the first time. Two minutes later, he was again inspired as he corkscrewed his way through to set up a try for Jordan. His efforts certainly contributed to the road to Wembley where he celebrated his thirtieth birthday at Crystal Palace the day before the final. Again, he was to figure in a defining moment. Midway through the first half, Barrow were leading 7-2 when Burgess, the Barrow winger, had been put clear in his own half and was streaking away over the half-way line. Wrigglesworth raced across and as Burgess attempted to outstrip him on the outside, Wrigglesworth launched himself in a superb ankle tackle to bring him down on the 25-yard line and save a certain try. Many consider that if Barrow had increased their lead then, it could have affected the result. Wrigglesworth then showed his attacking ability with a 50-yard run, one of the best of the game.

In a fantastic season in which he made 34 appearances, Wrigglesworth added a sparkle to the team. He decided to carry on into the next season 1967/68 and scored three tries in the opening four games and relished another impressive season. After four appearances in August 1968, he decided to retire and in 1970 he was appointed assistant player/coach. Not only did he pass on his experience to the 'A' team, but he guided them to the Yorkshire Senior Competition Championship in 1972.

In a comparatively short career, Wrigglesworth's impact was tremendous. His natural enthusiasm and flair in both attack and defence, as he rolled his sleeves up and his stockings down, were infectious. He was always eager to be in the action, and would come in to take the ball to relieve the forwards, at a time when this ploy was almost unheard of. Described as one of the pluckiest players in the game, I remember taking him to hospital from the Warrington game on 22 October 1966 with a horribly torn upper lip which had to be stitched together. He only missed one game before he returned to the fray!

Total appearances: 63 (+2)   Tries: 11   Goals: 1   Points: 35